Susan Long
28 Dalkeith Road
Dulwich
London SE21 8LS

DO-IT-YOURSELF CONVEYANCING

Here is a step-by-step guide to conveyancing procedure, sufficient to enable the layman to deal with a straightforward transaction. Care has been taken to highlight the legal problems that might be met, thus enabling the reader to identify that minority of transactions which are complex and where expert assistance should be sought. However, neither the author nor the publishers can accept any liability whatsoever for any loss arising from the use of this book in any particular case.

This book reflects conveyancing law and procedure as at 1 June 1978.

DO-IT-YOURSELF CONVEYANCING

A Practical Guide to
Handling The Legal Side Of
Buying And Selling A House

Robert T. Steele

DAVID & CHARLES
Newton Abbot   London   North Pomfret (Vt)

To my wife Catherine,
for the idea and the encouragement

British Library Cataloguing in Publication Data

Steele, Robert T
  Do-it-yourself conveyancing.
  1. Conveyancing – England – Amateurs' manuals
  I. Title
  346'.42'0438   KD979.5

  ISBN 0–7153–7676–4

Printed in Great Britain by
A. Wheaton & Co. Ltd., Exeter
for David & Charles (Publishers) Limited
Brunel House   Newton Abbot   Devon

Published in the United States of America
by David & Charles Inc
North Pomfret   Vermont 05053   USA

Contents

Part I: The Ground Rules

Introduction

The Purpose of This Book

This book explains the legal formalities involved in buying or selling a house in England or Wales (but not Scotland where a different system of law applies). It sets down the steps which must be taken and details the procedure which must be adopted. Sufficient information is given to enable the reader to deal with a straightforward domestic conveyancing transaction.

In being your own conveyancer, you will save yourself considerable expense. Unfortunately, there are some expenses that you are bound to incur whether or not you employ a solicitor. Thus, in buying property, you will still have to pay approximately £10 in Registry enquiry fees. Also, it may be necessary to register the transaction at HM Land Registry, in which case fees at the approximate rate of £2 for every £1,000 of purchase price are payable. Further, if you are paying a price in excess of £15,000 for property, government tax at the rate of ½ per cent on the purchase price will be payable. (This rate increases by ½ per cent in £5,000 steps up to a maximum of 2 per cent where the price exceeds £30,000.) In addition, if you are buying property with the aid of a building society loan, you must remember that you will have to pay their legal expenses.

However, despite this, you can still expect to save at least £100 in acting for yourself on the sale or purchase of a house.

This book details all the possible difficulties that may be encountered in a basic domestic transaction. The instruction given where such problems are met is usually 'seek legal advice'.

However, as you read through this book, do not let such instructions put you off. The odds are that they will not apply to you. Most domestic conveyancing is straightforward, and, provided you are careful and thorough, you are not likely to meet problems. But if you do find that you are getting out of your depth, place the matter in the hands of the experts.

This book is concerned solely with the legal aspects of conveyancing. It does not attempt to deal with the other practical problems that face a prospective seller or buyer. For example, it is assumed that you have satisfied yourself that you are able to finance the transaction and have chosen the most economic method of doing so. If this is not the case, you should not yet be contemplating being your own conveyancer.

Most people seem to assume that if they wish to buy or sell land they must employ a solicitor. This is not the case; 'doing-it-yourself' is perfectly legal. At the present time, what the law does prohibit is for someone other than a solicitor to do certain aspects of conveyancing work *for another, for reward.*

What Will You Need?

Conveyancing consists mainly of form-filling and letter writing. So, the first commodity you must possess is time to attend to these matters. In all, you can expect to have to spend up to, say, thirty hours in dealing with a purchase, and perhaps half that time in handling a sale.

All conveyancing documentation is typewritten so you must have access to a typewriter.

You will also need a file or folder in which to keep all the papers, a clip or tag by means of which all the correspondence can be held together, and a modest supply (fifty sheets or so) of plain white typing paper (A4 size is best). You should always place on your file a carbon copy of every letter that you write, so you will also need a similar number of sheets of copy paper, and some carbon paper.

Thus equipped, you are ready to proceed. Later, you will also need various printed forms and you will be told when and how to obtain them.

Before you Start

In preliminary preparation, you should read the whole of Part I of this book where the general procedure is outlined. Also, before you attempt some particular part of the conveyancing procedure, you must read the complete portion of this book that explains when, and how, that step is to be taken.

If you are buying, you will only be concerned with Parts I and II of this book; if you are selling, only Parts I and III. If you are proposing to act for yourself on a simultaneous sale and purchase, you will be referring to the whole book. In particular, before you start, you must have read Chapter 13 which deals with the special problems of co-ordinating a simultaneous sale and purchase.

1 General Outline of a Conveyancing Transaction

What is it all about?

In principle, buying or selling a house is no different from buying or selling anything else. A buyer is concerned to know precisely what he is being offered, how he can be sure that the seller is the owner of what he is offering for sale, and how ownership can be acquired.

In law, it is only possible for a person to own land in one of two ways: he may be a freeholder, or a leaseholder. A freehold interest is one which continues indefinitely, but a leasehold interest lasts only for the length of time specified by the document, the lease, by which it was granted. In broad terms, ownership of land includes the ownership of everything on, over, or under it. So, in buying land, one is also buying any house on it.

It is possible for a person to have an interest in property other than one of the two legal interests mentioned above, for example, the interests of a beneficiary under a will. However, no attempt is made in this book to consider transactions dealing with such interests.

It is most unlikely that the rights of a freeholder or leaseholder will be free from restriction. For example, he may well find that he is unable to use the property for some particular purpose, eg, because of a restrictive covenant in the deeds, or some local planning restriction. Therefore, during the course of the transaction, the purchaser is concerned not only to see that the vendor owns the land, but also to ascertain precisely what that ownership is subject to.

Proof of Ownership

It is not sufficient for a person to say that he owns property. He must be able to prove that he does. How this is done depends upon whether his rights as owner are 'registered' or 'unregistered'.

(i) *Unregistered title*—Where title to property is unregistered, a person proves his ownership by producing deeds. Deeds are documents which are signed, sealed, and delivered. By such a document, an owner of land states that he transfers his legal ownership to another. So, a person proves he owns land by producing a series of deeds which shows a chain of ownership leading to him.

(ii) *Registered title*—If the title to property has been 'registered', proof of ownership is greatly simplified. A person with an unregistered title obtains a registered title by proving his owner-ship to the Chief Land Registrar who will then register that person as proprietor. Once such registration has been completed, it is no longer necessary for future purchasers to investigate the seller's title to that property by examination of the deeds.

The Procedure in Outline

It is usually the vendor who takes the initiative in a conveyancing transaction by advertising his property for sale. All being well, a prospective buyer will respond, request to view the property and agree, in principle, to buy at a particular price. Then, with a view to reaching a firm agreement, the vendor will submit to the purchaser a 'draft contract' setting out in detail what the vendor has to sell and the terms on which he is prepared to sell it.

Before he makes himself legally liable to buy, the purchaser will read through the draft contract and will then make enquiries of the Local Authority in relation to such matters as, eg, planning restrictions ('making the local search'). The purchaser will also make certain other searches and submit to the vendor printed questions requesting information about the property, eg, as to boundaries, dry rot, etc.

If the buyer is pleased with what he learns of the property and is sure that he can finance the transaction, a removal date one month or so ahead will be agreed and the parties will sign the contract. This will normally require the purchaser to pay a 10 per cent deposit.

From the time of the initial negotiations, to the time when contracts are signed, is, on average, about one month.

At the outset, the seller and buyer are merely taken to be expressing a general intention to proceed to more formal negotiations which may result in the making of a legal contract. The initial agreement to proceed is 'subject to contract'. Either party is at liberty to decide not to go ahead with the transaction and, in so doing, will incur no liability.

Why must the agreement be in writing? The reason is that the law requires that, if a person is to have a contract involving land enforced against him, he must have signed something. So, in practice, to ensure that the arrangement will be legally enforceable, a formal written contract is prepared in duplicate and each party signs one copy of it and hands that to the other. This process is known as 'exchange of contracts'.

After contracts have been exchanged, the vendor will give to the purchaser a copy of his title documents which the purchaser will study to see if the vendor appears to own what he has agreed to sell.

Having made this investigation of the vendor's title, the purchaser will raise 'requisitions on title', that is, he will complete a form putting questions to the vendor requesting an explanation of any apparent defect in title. When any problems have been resolved, the purchaser will prepare the draft, or first rough copy, of the document which will transfer ownership to him. When this draft has been approved by the vendor, the purchaser will prepare the formal purchase deed from it (in legal jargon, he will 'engross' the purchase deed). The engrossed deed will be signed by the purchaser and then sent to the vendor for him to sign in readiness for completion.

Before he hands over his money, the buyer will make a

GENERAL OUTLINE OF A CONVEYANCING TRANSACTION

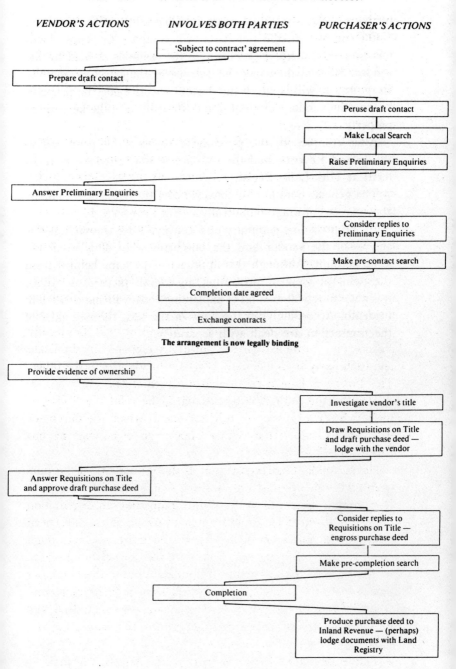

Fig 1

further search for information on liabilities affecting the property.

On completion, the purchaser will compare the copy documents of title in his possession with the originals as held by the vendor. He will then pay the balance of the purchase monies. In return, he will be given the document conveying the property to him, the vendor's original title documents, and the keys to the property.

After completion, the purchase deed must be produced to the Inland Revenue and the transaction may need to be registered at HM Land Registry.

The general outline of a conveyancing transaction as detailed above is set out diagrammatically in Fig 1 on page 13.

In the preceding summary of a conveyancing transaction, the actions of the vendor and the purchaser were detailed in the same account. Although this approach is perhaps helpful from the point of view of presenting an overall picture of events, it is not a practical method of explaining conveyancing procedure in depth. Accordingly, in the body of the text, the two sides of the transaction are dealt with separately.

2 The Language Explained

The purpose of this chapter is to provide a glossary of the main legal terms which you are likely to encounter in dealing with a conveyancing transaction. You will be able to refer to it when you are faced with some strange word. It is sufficiently extensive to be adequate for most of your needs. However, it cannot be over-emphasised that, if you do not understand the meaning of a particular document, or are unsure as to what it will accomplish, you should seek expert assistance.

Glossary

Absolute title the highest quality of ownership in land recognised by the system of registration of title.

Abstract of title a summary (usually by means of typed or photographed copies) of the documents and facts showing ownership.

Assignment a disposal or transfer of property. The word is most commonly used in relation to the transfer of the benefit of a lease, which will be accomplished by a deed called 'an assignment'.

Beneficial owner a person owning land and entitled to it for his own benefit.

Beneficiary a person who is entitled to benefit under a trust or will.

Caution in relation to registered land, an entry on the Register protecting an interest of a third party.

Charge, a a liability burdening land securing the payment of money, eg, a mortgage.

Charge by way of Legal Mortgage/Legal Charge a mortgage.

Consideration the price paid for something done or promised.

Conveyance a document transferring the ownership of property. The word is particularly used to describe a deed transferring the freehold interest.

Counterpart (particularly in relation to leases)—it is common for a lease to be prepared in duplicate with the intention that the landlord and the tenant should each sign one copy and that these should then be exchanged. The part, or copy, signed by the person granting the lease is called the 'original', and the part signed by the tenant is called the 'counterpart'.

Covenant a promise given by deed.

Easement a right owned by one landowner over the land of another, eg, a right of way.

Estate (a) *in land* the extent of a person's ownership, eg, freehold or leasehold;
(b) *of a deceased person* all the property owned by that person at his death.

Execute (a) the signing of a document;
(b) the enforcement of a decision of the court, eg, by the seizure of the wrongdoer's goods to pay the debt or compensation due.

Fee simple the interest owned by a legal freeholder.

Floating charge a charge on all the assets of a company which does not affect the company's power of disposal unless and until the charge crystalises, ie, becomes payable.

Joint and several together as one, and also separately, eg, of liability under a covenant.

Joint tenants co-owners of land. When one of them dies, his rights of ownership pass to the survivor/s (contrast tenancy in common).

Mortgage to give to a lender important rights over property, including the power of sale, as security for a loan.

Overriding interests an interest of a third party in registered land which binds the owner even though there is no note of it on the Register, eg, the rights of a person in actual occupation of the land.

Private treaty a sale not by auction.

Rent a periodic payment in respect of land, eg,
    (a) *ground rent* the sum payable under a lease;
    (b) *chief rent, or rentcharge* rent payable in respect of freehold property.

Restrictive covenant a covenant, ie, a promise under seal, restricting the use of land.

Root of title the document from which a vendor's ownership is traced.

Seisin/seised possession of land as freeholder.

Tenancy in common where two or more people are entitled, eg, to the proceeds of sale in land, in distinct shares. On the death of one, his interest will not pass to the survivor/s but will be part of his estate.

Tenure the terms on which land is held, eg, freehold or leasehold.

Title the evidence of a person's right to land.

Trust where property is transferred to a person on the understanding that he will apply it for some particular purpose, eg, 'to A *on trust* for my wife and daughter'.

Trust for sale a trust which requires the trustees to sell the property. Co-owners of land will hold it as joint tenants on trust for sale (but with power to postpone sale), perhaps for the benefit of themselves as joint tenants.

Vacating receipt an endorsement on a mortgage stating that it has been paid off.

Part II : Buying

3 The Initial Negotiations

In looking round the property, do not allow yourself to be rushed from room to room, but take your time to examine the whole fabric of the house. You may consider it necessary to ask for the carpets to be lifted, or furniture moved, if you feel that these might obscure some defect.

Unless you are yourself qualified to pass judgement on the physical condition of the property, you would be well advised to obtain a surveyor's report, particularly in the case of older houses. (If you are buying the property with the aid of a mortgage, the lender will undoubtedly wish to have the property surveyed, but you will not be allowed to see the report.)

You should inspect the grounds, looking particularly for any signs which might indicate that some third person claims rights over the property, eg, well worn tracks at the bottom of the garden.

It is also important that you are clear as to what fixtures and fittings are to be included in the sale. Ask the vendor if he intends to remove any TV aerial, electrical fittings, fitted shelves, etc. Inquire whether the property is freehold or leasehold, whether there are any restrictions affecting the use of the property (eg, prohibiting the erection of fences, or the keeping of animals, caravans, etc), and also, in the case of leasehold property, how long the lease has to run, and what the rent is.

Should you still find the property attractive, then you can start to talk in terms of a price. If the vendor will accept what you offer, ask him whether he will be instructing a solicitor.

Where this is his intention, suggest that he notifies the solicitor of the proposed sale, and request details of that person's name and address.

Although it is not usual for the initial negotiations to produce an agreement in the strict legal sense, it is possible for this to be the result where the parties are sufficiently firm and definite in their intention. You must *not* be so definite in your intention to buy until you have completed all the usual pre-contract enquiries as detailed in Chapter 4 of this book.

Throughout the initial negotiations, be careful to make it quite clear that any offer you make is conditional upon the usual enquiries being made, and a formal contract being entered into. Use the words 'subject to contract', if you wish. In any event, an agreement involving land cannot normally be enforced against a person unless he has put his signature to some document, so just be sure you *do not sign anything*, whether it be a letter, estate agent's form, or anything else, which states that you have agreed, unconditionally, to buy a house, unless and until you have taken all the appropriate steps specified in the check-list on page 47.

If the property is being sold through an estate agent, he may well be reluctant to recommend acceptance of your offer (as a ploy to induce you perhaps to make a higher one). Before he will treat the property as 'sold subject to contract' he will clearly wish you to satisfy him that you can finance the purchase. He might also suggest that you pay him a 'holding deposit'. However, there is no legal force in paying such a deposit and the house can still be sold elsewhere, so pay as little as you can.

If you are proposing to buy the house with the assistance of a building society loan, you should now make application for an advance. To ascertain whether the property you are considering buying is a good enough security for the loan requested, the building society will require the property to be surveyed and valued, at your expense.

In the normal domestic conveyancing transaction the situation is as follows. The property concerned is a private dwelling-house set in its own grounds; it is owned by a husband, or husband and wife jointly; there is no one other than the owner(s) and his (their) family in occupation; the whole of the property is being sold, and with vacant possession.

It is only in the case of such a straightforward case that the layman should attempt to be his own conveyancer. This book will not equip you to deal with the more complicated situations that are sometimes encountered; for example, in any of the following cases:

1 Where the property is not being sold for its proper market value, eg, in the case of gifts, and other dispositions between relatives.

2 Where the property is being sold by auction.

3 Where the owner does not live on the premises and yet they appear to be occupied.

4 Where the property is being sold subject to the occupation of tenants.

5 Where the owner is a company and not a private individual.

6 Where the property is a new house in the course of construction.

7 The sale of a flat.

In any case out of the ordinary, do not proceed without expert advice.

4 Before You Sign the Contract

The Steps to be Taken

Between the initial negotiations and exchange of contracts you must attend to the following matters:

1 Obtain your pre-contract conveyancing forms.
2 Make a local search.
3 Obtain and peruse the draft contract.
4 Raise preliminary enquiries.
5 Make a search in the Land Charges Registry.
6 Make a search of the index map at HM Land Registry.

A typical timetable of when these events might take place is as follows:

Day 1   Agree to buy 'subject to contract'.
Day 2   Order pre-contract conveyancing forms.
         Write to the vendor's solicitor requesting a draft contract for approval.

Day 6 Pre-contract conveyancing forms received.
Send off local search form.
Day 7 Draft contract received and perused.
Make your preliminary enquiries.
Day 12 Receive replies to preliminary enquiries.
Approve draft contract.
Send off land charges search form.
Send off your index map search form.
Day 16 Receive result of land charges search.
Receive result of index map search.
Day 20 Receive result of local search.
Day 23 Exchange contracts.

Obtaining Your Pre-Contract Conveyancing Forms

The forms that you will need before exchange of contracts are as follows:

1 *Local Search*—one copy of form L.L.C.I. published by HMSO.

2 *Additional Enquiries of Local Authority*—two copies of either Oyez Publishing Ltd, form CON 29 ENGLAND AND WALES (EXCLUDING LONDON) (where the property you are buying is outside the London area), or form CON 29 LONDON (where the property is in the area of a London borough council or the Corporation of London).

3 *Preliminary Enquiries*—two copies of Oyez Publishing Ltd, form CON 29 (LONG).

4 *Land Charges Search*—one copy of form LAND CHARGES K15 published by HMSO.

5 *Land Registry Index Map Search*—one copy of Oyez Publishing Ltd, or HMSO form LAND REGISTRY 96.

Each of these forms costs only a few pence and they can all be obtained from any branch of Oyez Stationery Ltd, (for the addresses see page 153), or, if you prefer, you can obtain those detailed in 1, 4, and 5, above, from any HMSO bookshop or agent.

Obtaining the Draft Contract

We will be assuming for the sake of explaining conveyancing procedure that the vendor is legally represented. If this is not the case, then simply treat all references to 'the vendor's solicitor' as references to 'the vendor' personally.

To obtain the draft contract, write to the vendor's solicitor giving the full address of the property concerned and stating that you have agreed *subject to contract* to buy at a particular price from his client (and name the vendor). Say that you will be handling the matter personally and request a draft contract for approval as soon as possible.

Making the Local Search

Local authorities keep details of charges and restrictions affecting land in their area. In making a local search, a prospective purchaser is asking the local authority for information about the land he is considering buying. This he does by sending to the local authority completed forms L.L.C.I., and CON 29 ENGLAND AND WALES (EXCLUDING LONDON) (or CON 29 LONDON, where the house is in the area of a London borough council, or the Corporation of London) in duplicate, with the appropriate fee. You should make your local search as soon as you receive the conveyancing forms.

Form L.L.C.I. has its own duplicate attached. The form and duplicate should be addressed to the local district (not county) council for the area in which the property is situated, and completed as illustrated in Fig 2 on page 25.

It is best to enclose a plan of the property (in duplicate) with your application unless the postal address clearly identifies the land (see note (9) on the front page of the CON 29 form). The vendor's solicitor will undoubtedly be able to supply two copies of a deed plan for this purpose. At present, the fee for a L.L.C.I. search is £1.25.

The questions on the CON 29 form are divided into two parts. The local authority will only answer a question in Part II of

Form LLCI. *(Local Land Charges Rules 1977 Schedule 1, Form C)*

Official Number_____
(To be completed by the registering authority)

The duplicate of this form must also be completed:
a carbon copy will suffice

For directions, notes and fees see overleaf

Insert name and address of registering authority in space below

> NEWTOWN DISTRICT COUNCIL,
> TOWN HALL,
> NEWTOWN,
> BLANKSHIRE.

Register of local land charges

Requisition for search and official certificate of search

fold

Requisition for search
(A separate requisition must be made in respect of each parcel of land except as explained overleaf)

An official search is required in ~~Part(s)~~ _____
the register of local land charges kept by the clerk of the above-named registering authority for subsisting registrations against the land [defined in the attached plan and]² described below.

Description of land sufficient to enable it to be identified

1, MAIN STREET, NEWTOWN, BLANKSHIRE.

Name and address to which certificate is to be sent

> MR. M. E. PURCHASER,
> PIER HOTEL,
> WIGAN,
> LANCASHIRE.

Signature of applicant *(or his solicitor)*

M. E. Purchaser.

Date

__7th July 1978__

Telephone number

-

Reference

-

Enclosure
Cheque/~~Money Order/Postal Order/Giro~~   £1.25

Official certificate of search

It is hereby certified that the search requested above reveals no subsisting registrations³

or the _____ registrations described in the Schedule hereto³ up to and including the date of this certificate.

Signed...

On behalf of... 4

Date

To be completed by authorised officer

1 Delete if inappropriate. Otherwise insert Part(s) in which search is required.

2 Delete if inappropriate. (A plan should be furnished in duplicate if it is desired that a copy should be returned.)

3 Delete inapplicable words. (The Parts of the Schedule should be securely attached to the certificate and the number of registrations disclosed should be inserted in the space provided. Only Parts which disclose subsisting registrations should be sent.)

4 Insert name of registering authority.

C175

Fig 2

the form if the applicant puts his initials alongside it. In the normal domestic conveyancing transaction it is not necessary to ask any of these optional questions as they relate to such matters as, eg, Green Belt areas, and classification of buildings as being of special architectural or historic interest. However, if you are in any doubt as to whether any of these questions might be applicable, a visit to the local authority offices will usually prove helpful.

The front page of the enquiries form should be completed, signed and dated. In the space for fees (assuming that you are not asking any of the questions in Part II of the form) insert £4.50.

You must also complete question 1 on page 2 of the form with the name(s) of the road(s) on which the property abuts.

The request for copies of planning permissions at the end of enquiry 14 on the London councils form can usually be deleted as the vendor will normally supply a copy of such when he replies to your preliminary enquiries.

The completed forms, and any plans, should be sent to the local authority concerned, with your remittance for the total fee payable, which will usually be £5.75.

As to the result of the search, see page 41.

Perusing the Draft Contract

Where there is a solicitor acting for the vendor, the draft contract will almost certainly consist of a printed standard form of contract, the blank spaces of which have been completed with the appropriate details of the property concerned.

This form will usually be the Law Society contract for sale, or the contract by reference to the National Conditions of Sale. Both of these forms are four-page documents which have conditions set out in small print on the inside. Both are headed on the front page with their title. The Law Society contract is on buff-coloured paper, the National Conditions of Sale on pale blue. Sometimes, a solicitor will use a standard form of contract prepared by a local law society or by his own firm. If the vendor is not legally represented, the contract may simply consist of a typed document.

The draft contract is being sent to you for you to approve, ie, for you to indicate whether or not you will be prepared to commit yourself to buy on the terms there stated.

The vendor's solicitor will have prepared the draft contract in duplicate and he may have sent both copies to you. If this is the case, it is intended that you should return the top copy to him when you signify your approval in due course. If you were supplied with only one copy of the draft contract, then this will be retained by you, the vendor's solicitor having kept one copy for use by his client. If you and the vendor's solicitor agree some change in the proposed terms of the sale, then the two parts of the draft contract must be altered accordingly.

When you receive the draft contract you must read it through very carefully, making notes of any matters which you think require further clarification. Pay particular attention to the following matters:

1 *Names of the parties* If there are to be joint owners of the house, eg, husband and wife, both should be mentioned as purchasers.

2 *Purchase price* This should be what you agreed to pay.

3 *Physical description of the property* This will often commence with the words 'All That'. The description should adequately identify the land you wish to buy, eg, 'the house and garden known as 1 Main Street, Newtown, Blankshire'. In the case of a sale of property with registered title the description will refer to the title number allotted to it. The description may make some mention of a plan or of particular colouring on a plan. Look at the copy of the plan supplied to you to see that it accurately represents what you wish to buy. If necessary, arrange to have another look at the land. If the copy plan supplied has not been 'edged red' or 'coloured blue' like the original, it should be returned to the vendor's solicitor.

The contract may state that the house is being sold with the benefit of certain specific rights, eg, a right of way over someone else's land. It takes legal training to know whether or not, as owner of the property, you will have the legal right to enjoy that benefit. Thus, where the rights mentioned are such that they will be important to you if you buy the house, you must seek expert advice. There is one exception to this. Where title to the property is registered, if the owner of the property is legally entitled to the benefit of some specific right, this will normally be included as part of the description of the property as given in the Register, Part A, Property Register. Ask the vendor's solicitor for a copy of the Register if you have not already been supplied with one. (As to what the Register looks like, see pages 64 and 65). Where the right is protected by such registration, there is no need to take legal advice concerning its validity.

4 *Land with registered title* If the contract states that title to the property is registered, some indication will normally be given as to the quality of title possessed by the vendor, eg, 'registered with absolute title'. If the vendor's title is only 'qualified' or 'possessory', you should seek legal advice. In the case of registered leasehold title, 'good leasehold' title is quite acceptable provided that the lease concerned is not less than fifteen years old.

5 *Matters which the property is being sold subject to* Take particular care to ascertain precisely what the property is subject to. Restrictive and other covenants, exceptions and reservations, rights, and agreements and declarations (and, in the case of leasehold property, the terms of the lease and the rent reserved by it) are quite normal things to affect a property, but clearly you will need to know the exact nature of them. If the contract does not set such matters out in full (eg, does not quote the covenant in full) but simply refers to the document in which they are contained, eg, a conveyance, or the Land Registry Register, then you will normally be supplied with a copy of that document along with the draft contract. If this is not the case, be sure to request a copy of the document. Such documents should be read carefully so that you are sure that you are aware of just what is on offer.

When you are buying leasehold property, you must familiarise yourself with the terms of the lease. From a general conveyancing point of view, watch for a clause which stipulates that the landlord must consent to any sale of the benefit of the lease, or be given notice of any intended assignment. Should the lease contain such a provision, make a note to ask for confirmation that the landlord's written consent (when required) will be obtained before contracts are exchanged, or that evidence of service of the notice will be handed over on completion.

If the contract states that the property is being sold subject to some matter of a description not mentioned above, eg, to a charge, legal charge, or mortgage, you should obtain legal advice before proceeding.

6 *'The vendor sells as . . .'* The vendor(s) will normally sell 'as Beneficial Owner' or 'as Trustees'. If the contract states that the vendor sells in some other capacity you will have to place the matter in expert hands.

7 *Title* Except where the title to the property is registered, there will be a clause in the contract stating that the vendor's title 'shall commence with . . .'. In the case of freehold property, this clause should specify a conveyance of the land dated at least fifteen years previously. If it does not, seek expert advice. In the case of leasehold property, title will commence with the lease. If the lease is less than fifteen years old some evidence of the prior freehold title going back at least that far should be offered.

8 *Tenure* The contract will specify whether the vendor is selling the freehold or leasehold interest. If the leasehold is being sold, note the length of the term of years granted and the rent payable.

9 *Completion date* There is usually a clause stating that 'completion will take place on ....19.......' This space is left blank until exchange of contracts.

10 *Interest* The contract normally specifies a particular rate of interest for the purposes of the contract. The figure stated might be anything from 10–15 per cent. This provision relates to one of the small-print conditions of the contract which allows the

vendor to charge you interest on the amount of the purchase price remaining to be paid when, eg, you take possession before completion, or completion is delayed.

11 *Other clauses* Apart from the small-print conditions of the contract, you may find that the contract includes some additional clause of a description not discussed above, eg, saying that the price includes carpets or curtains. From the legal standpoint, there is nothing unusual about such a provision. It is simply a question of whether or not you wish to buy on those terms.

On the other hand, if the clause in question states, for example, that the vendor's title to the house is defective in some way and requires you to accept it without question or objection, or that the property is being sold subject to some other person's rights of occupation, you must obtain expert assistance.

One of the clauses of the contract will usually incorporate some standard form of general conditions such as the Law Society Conditions of Sale, or the National Conditions of Sale. These will often be set out in full on the inside pages of the contract. If they are not, ask the vendor's solicitor to supply a copy of them. Such standard conditions of sale are part of the contract and should be read by you.

Preliminary Enquiries

As soon as you have completed your perusal of the draft contract, you should raise your preliminary enquiries (or 'enquiries before contract' as they are sometimes called) by completing and sending to the vendor's solicitor form CON 29 (Long) in duplicate. The purpose of the preliminary enquiries is to obtain information about the property which is important to you as a prospective purchaser, and to resolve any queries raised by your perusal of the draft contract.

On the three dotted lines at the top of the front page of the form you should insert, respectively, the address of the property, the name(s) of the vendor(s), and your name(s) as purchaser(s).

The forms should be signed and dated in the left-hand column immediately above the first enquiry. There is space on the last two pages for additional enquiries and, in that space, you should type appropriate questions to cover any specific queries you have with regard to the draft contract or concerning the property generally.

Where the title to the property that you are considering buying is *not* registered (see the draft contract), the following additional question should be added to the form, word for word :

Please supply a list of the names and periods of ownership of all estate owners of the property (including, where the property is leasehold, the owners of the superior title/titles), since 1st January 1926, other than those in respect of which the vendor will be able to produce on completion a certificate of search obtained within the appropriate period of protection prior to their disposing of the land.

You will need this information to enable you to make a land charges search later.

Also, whether or not title is registered, if you are in any doubt as to whether the property is in an area of coal mining, you should ask the following question :

Is the property in an area of coal mining, and, if so, is it subject to subsidence?

If you know that the property is in an area of coal mining, write to the local National Coal Board Area Office for further details of workings and subsidence.

The completed forms should be sent to the vendor's solicitor, preferably with a covering letter.

In due course he will return one copy of the form with replies (having retained the other copy for his file). The replies should be considered carefully. They must not be vague and unspecific, or be those of the vendor's solicitor rather than the vendor where the subject of the enquiry is a matter known only to the vendor, eg, disputes with neighbours. If a reply is unacceptable, refer it back to the vendor's solicitor. Most of the replies will be self-explanatory, but the following points should be noted in relation to the standard enquiries :

1 *Boundaries* With older properties, ownership of boundary walls and fences is often unclear. With newer houses, the deeds are usually specific as to such matters.

2 *Disputes* If the answer is 'yes', you should request further information on which to base your decision as to whether or not to proceed.

4 *Guarantees* If there is a National House-Building Council certificate and agreement, you should ask the vendor's solicitor to agree to the inclusion of the following clause in the contract :

> On completion the vendor will hand over the NHBC Protection Certificate in respect of the property and will assign to the purchaser the benefit of the House Purchaser's Agreement.

6 *Shared facilities* If there are any shared facilities of an essential nature, you should seek expert assistance so as to be sure that you will obtain the full legal benefit of them (see page 27).

7 *Adverse rights* If there are any such adverse rights, you will be buying subject to them. The choice is yours!

8 *Restrictions* All restrictions affecting the property should have been observed. If this does not appear to be the case, seek legal advice.

9 *Planning* If there has been any development, eg, change of use, building works, etc, on the property in the last four years, you should ask the vendor for evidence that planning permission was obtained, or was not necessary. Where conditions were imposed by any planning permission, these must have been met.

10 *Development Land Tax* If the answer is 'yes', take legal advice.

11 *Fixtures and Fittings* All fixtures, ie, things attached to and forming part of the land, will be included in the sale unless expressly excluded. Where you have agreed to buy, eg, carpets or curtains, it is best to have a special clause in the contract stating that they are included in the sale and stipulating the price to be paid for them.

19 *Reversionary title* The answer may well be 'no', but if the lease is at least fifteen years old this is no cause for alarm. The other leasehold enquiries are quite straightforward, but if the answer to enquiry 16 indicates that the covenants in the lease have been broken, seek legal advice.

Estate owners In response to the additional enquiry that you may have raised asking for a list of the owners of the property since 1 January 1926, the reply may indicate that such information cannot be given in respect of the period before the root of title specified in the contract. Such a reply is quite acceptable as the vendor may well have no knowledge of dealings with the land prior to that time.

Approving the Draft Contract

When you have read through the draft contract and have resolved any outstanding points thereon by your preliminary enquiries, you are in a position to write to the vendor's solicitor (returning one copy of the draft contract to him if you have both) telling him that you 'approve the draft contract'. This simply means that you give your broad approval to the terms on which the vendor is prepared to sell the property. It in no way commits you to buy on those terms because, in approving it, you do *not* sign the contract.

Before approving the contract, agree the inclusion of any extra clauses, eg, dealing with any furniture included in the sale, or NHBC Agreement.

Land Charges Search

Besides the Register of Local Land Charges, maintained by the local authority, there is another register of charges which concerns land, the central Land Charges Department, at Plymouth.

You should make a search of this Register immediately after you receive the replies to your preliminary enquiries, by completing the Land Charges Act 1972 form K15.

On the form there are three main pieces of information that you need to give to the Registry; the names to be searched, the period of years you wish the search to cover, and the county.

Names to be searched. Where the title to the property is not registered, in your preliminary enquiries you will have asked the vendor's solicitor for a list of all owners of the property since 1 January 1926, except those for whom he can produce an official certificate of search. Your search now should be against the names supplied and also against the name of the vendor(s). Where title to the property is registered, the only name to search against is that of the vendor(s).

There are two lines allowed for each name; one for the forename(s), and one for the surname. Enter the appropriate details of the owner's full name. If that person is also known by some other name, eg, Francis and Frank, or the name has changed during the period of ownership, eg, on marriage, the two names should be treated separately. Sometimes it is not clear whether the middle name is a forename or a surname, eg, John Roberts Jones. Here the only safe course is to search against the two alternatives. If you do not know the full details of the name of a particular owner as it might appear on the Register, you must ask the vendor's solicitor for such information.

Where the person is known as 'Sir' or 'The Honourable' these titles can be omitted from the name for search purposes. Where a search is to be made against a peer, a bishop, a company, or a local authority, the words 'forename(s)' and 'surname' should be deleted and the name inserted commencing on the first line of the box and continuing on the second line if necessary.

If the six name spaces provided are not sufficient, you will have to obtain a further form, or forms.

The period of years. The period to be searched is the time during which the person concerned was an owner of the property, expressed in whole calendar years. For example, if a person was an owner from 13 March 1962, to 18 October 1971, you would put ┌─────┬─────┐ 1962 │ 1971 └─────┴─────┘. If you do not know when the period of ownership commenced put 1926 in the 'from' box; if you do not know when it ended, put the current year in the 'to' box. Where you are dealing with registered title and are simply searching against the name of the vendor(s) you should insert the current year in the 'to' box and a year six years prior to the current year in the 'from' box, eg, ┌─────┬─────┐ 1972 │ 1978 └─────┴─────┘.

County. Registrations in the central Land Charges Registry are grouped according to the county in which the land affected is situated. With boundary adjustments and local government reorganisation, the name of the county could well have changed. Thus you are asked to supply details of the present county and of any former county.

In relation to the county names prior to the local government reorganisation in 1974, it should be noted that, for the purposes of the index; Cambridgeshire included the Isle of Ely, Cornwall included the Isles of Scilly, Hampshire included the Isle of Wight, Huntingdonshire included Peterborough, Lincolnshire included the Parts of Holland, Kesteven and Lindsey, Suffolk included East and West Suffolk, Sussex included East and West Sussex, and Yorkshire included the three Ridings and the City of York.

For searches in respect of land in the London area, the county is Greater London. Prior to the formation of that area in 1965, the property may have been in Surrey, Kent, or Middlesex.

A search against the vendor(s) of land with registered title should give details of the county in which that person currently resides.

As to the remainder of the K15 form, the boxes 'description of land' and 'former description' should be left blank, as should the 'key number' box. Put your name and address, and the date in the appropriate place. There is no need to specify an 'address for despatch of certificate' if you wish it to be sent to your address as given on the form.

An example of a completed form K15 is given in Fig 3 on page 37.

Before you post the form, affix to its top right-hand corner Land Registry fee stamps to cover the fees payable. The search fee is (currently) 50p for each name to be searched. The stamps can be obtained from any Head Post Office. When you obtain your supply for the land charges search, purchase extra stamps to the value of £1 to cover the fee on the index map search that you will be making shortly. Also, while you are at the Post Office, ask for a copy of Inland Revenue form, Stamps L(A) 451, Particulars of Instruments Transferring or Leasing Land. You will be needing this form after completion.

In due course, you will receive the result of your search.

Where the search has revealed no subsisting entries the official certificate of result will be on form K17, and no further action will be required on your part.

Where the search has revealed entries registered against some or all of the names searched against, the certificate of result will be on form K18. There are two questions that you will need to consider in relation to each entry revealed : first, does the registration affect the property that you are considering buying, and second, if it does, what is its effect?

In relation to the first question, you need to appreciate that there could well be several people of the same name in the same area, and your search entry could relate to any one of them. Also, even if the land charge was registered against the person that you are interested in, he may have owned other property to which the land charge in fact relates. Further, since land charges are registered against owners, those registered against a person before he became an owner of the property or after he ceased to own it do not concern you.

Some of these difficulties will probably be resolved by the certificate of result itself since it will give details of the date of registration of the charge, a short description of the land affected, and the name and address of the person who created the charge.

If the details on the K18 are not sufficient to indicate con-

FORM K15   LAND CHARGES ACT 1972

APPLICATION FOR AN OFFICIAL SEARCH

NOT APPLICABLE TO REGISTERED LAND

Application is hereby made for an official search in the index to the registers kept
pursuant to the Land Charges Act 1972 for any subsisting entries in respect of the
under-mentioned particulars.

For Official Use Only			IMPORTANT:	Please read the notes overleaf before completing this form. No covering letter is required to accompany this application.		

		NAMES TO BE SEARCHED	PERIOD OF YEARS	
STX		Please use block letters	From	To
	Forename(s)	CHARLES JAMES EDWARD BLACK 8th EARL of	1926	1950
	Surname	NEWTOWN		
	Forename(s)	THE NEWTOWN R.D.C.	1950	1955
	Surname			
	Forename(s)	BEAUTIFUL BUILDERS CO LTD	1955	1960
	Surname			
	Forename(s)	JOHN WILLIAMS	1960	1968
	Surname	SMITH		
	Forename(s)	JOHN	1960	1968
	Surname	WILLIAMS SMITH		
	Forename(s)	ALBERT	1968	1978
	Surname	VENDOR		

COUNTY	GREATER MANCHESTER
FORMER COUNTY	LANCASHIRE
DESCRIPTION OF LAND (See note 7 overleaf)	
FORMER DESCRIPTION	

PARTICULARS OF APPLICANT		ADDRESS FOR DESPATCH OF CERTIFICATE (Leave blank if certificate to be returned to applicant's address)
KEY NUMBER	NAME AND ADDRESS	
	MR. M.E. PURCHASER, PIER HOTEL, WIGAN, LANCASHIRE.	

Applicant's reference: —	Date 15.7.78.	FOR OFFICAL USE ONLY

Fig 3

clusively whether or not the entry does concern you, contact the vendor's solicitor and ask him if he has any knowledge of the matter. If necessary, he will be able to obtain additional information about the entry by requesting from the Land Charges Department 'an office copy of the entry', ie, a copy of the original application form for registration.

If the vendor's solicitor says that the entry does not relate but the circumstances are such that it is not beyond question that what he says is fact, it is usual to ask him to certify the certificate of result. This means that he writes on the K18, eg, 'I certify that this entry does not relate to the . . . (eg, Albert Vendor) . . . the owner of . . . (description of the property) . . .', or 'does not affect the property . . . (and its address) . . .', or whatever words are appropriate in the circumstances, and signs and dates his certification.

You may find that your certificate of result of search gives details of a particular type of charge corresponding to one of those mentioned later except for the fact that it has the prefix 'PN'. These letters stand for priority notice and they mean that an entry of the kind referred to was not actually registered at the date of the search but was about to be so. Unless there is some indication to suggest that the priority notice was not followed through with formal registration, you should treat priority notice entries in the same way as charges actually registered at the date of search.

So far as a search made against the vendor(s) of land with registered title is concerned, the only kinds of entries that you need concern yourself with are PA(B), and WO(B) entries which relate to the bankruptcy of a person. Any others can be ignored. If there is a land charge of the kind mentioned above registered against the name of the vendor, ask the vendor's solicitor whether the entry relates to his client.

If he informs you that the registration *does* relate to his client, then you must seek legal advice before proceeding. If he states that the entry refers, not to his client, but to some other person of the same name, ask him to confirm that, on exchange of contracts, he will certify the certificate of result to that effect. **Provided that he is prepared to do this, you will usually be** safe to proceed, but if he is not, take legal advice.

If the vendor of the registered land is not legally represented and an entry of the kind mentioned above is revealed against his name then, unless you are *absolutely sure* that the entry does not relate to him but to some other person of the same name, you must not proceed without first taking legal advice.

In relation to a search made against the owners of land with unregistered title, all the entries revealed are of concern to you but only those detailed below are likely to be encountered.

C(i) and C(iii) These relate to mortgages of the land. You will not normally be agreeing to buy subject to such matters, so you will wish to be sure that, either the entry does not relate to the property, or that it has been removed (or will be removed before you complete your purchase). For this purpose, you can accept the vendor's solicitor's certification that it does not relate, or his confirmation that it will be removed. He may say that he will deliver to you on completion a completed and signed form of application for cancellation of the land charge (form K11). This is just as good as having the registration removed and can be accepted. Similar evidence can be accepted from an unrepresented vendor, but, in addition, where he is alleging that the charge does not affect his property, you should ask him to supply you with an office copy of the entry before you agree to proceed. From an examination of this, it should be apparent whether or not what he says is correct. Where the assurances detailed above are not forthcoming, take legal advice before proceeding.

D(ii) This kind of entry is to protect a restrictive covenant. If the property is being sold subject to a restrictive covenant, all you need be sure of is that the registration in fact relates to the particular covenant disclosed by the vendor. A certificate to this effect from the vendor's solicitor is usually accepted as being sufficient for this purpose. Where the vendor is not legally represented, you should ask for an office copy of the entry so that you can identify the covenant for yourself. If it is clearly the one referred to in the contract, then there is no need to ask the vendor to certify the search.

Where it is alleged that the entry does not affect the property, you should only proceed if the vendor's solicitor (or the vendor personally, if he is unrepresented) is prepared to certify the certificate of result. In addition, insist that an unrepresented vendor supply you with an office copy of the entry so that you can check for yourself that what he says appears to be true.

F By such an entry, a spouse who does not own the matrimonial home protects his or her right to occupy it.

The details of the entry as given in the search result may not be sufficient to convince you that the registration does not concern you. If this is the case, refer the matter to the vendor's solicitor. If he is prepared to certify that the entry does not relate to the property that you are buying, this can usually be accepted. In addition to the certificate, an unrepresented vendor should be asked to supply an office copy of the entry to confirm what he says.

If the registration does affect the property then, subject to what is said in the next paragraph, you must not proceed until it is removed and the cancellation certificate is shown to you.

The registration, if there is one, will usually be against the name of the vendor. In such cases, you can safely proceed if you are given a letter signed by the person entitled to the benefit of the rights of occupation, ie, the vendor's spouse, stating that he or she agrees to the sale, and, on completion, will give you a signed form of application for cancellation of the registration (form K13).

PA, PA(B), WO, WO(B), D of A As mentioned previously, these entries normally relate to the insolvency of the owner. If such a registration is revealed, you should only proceed if the vendor's solicitor is prepared to certify that it does not affect the property. If he is not able to give this certificate, seek legal advice before proceeding. Where the vendor is unrepresented and such an entry is registered against him, *do not proceed* without first obtaining legal advice.

Where you come across an entry of a type not described above, seek expert assistance.

Index Map Search

This search of the index map at HM Land Registry is made by completing Land Registry form 96. In the appropriate spaces on the top half of the form, put your name and address, details of the property, and the date. It is not necessary to send a plan with the search request if the postal address is sufficient to identify the property.

Land Registry fee stamps for £1^2 should be affixed to the top right-hand corner of the form (or, alternatively, the fee may be paid by postal order). The form should then be signed, and sent to the district Land Registry for the area, as detailed on the reverse of the form.

The form will be returned to you with the result of the search endorsed on the lower half of the front page.

An example of how the form might be completed and how the search result might appear in the case of unregistered property is given in Fig 4 on page 42.

The information given by the result of the search should correspond with what the vendor has told you about the property, eg, that title is registered freehold or leasehold, and the title number. If there is any discrepancy, you must ask the vendor's solicitor for an explanation. In particular, if the search indicates that title is registered and yet you have been told that the vendor is selling unregistered title, or the search discloses that the property is subject to a caution against first registration, or to a priority notice, take legal advice.

Result of Local Search

The local search consisted of the request for an official certificate of search, and the additional enquiries. The result of these will be given by the local authority returning to you one copy of each of the forms that you lodged.

The result of your application for an official certificate of search will be endorsed on the lower portion of the form L.L.C.I. It will be signed on behalf of the local authority and will indicate that

APPLICATION FOR AN OFFICIAL SEARCH OF THE INDEX MAP

Please read the notes overleaf

1/96

[USE
BLOCK
LETTERS]

MR. M. E. PURCHASER,
PIER HOTEL,
WIGAN, LANCASHIRE.

Reference _____ -

Telephone no. _____ -

hereby apply, under rule 286 of the Land Registration Rules, 1925, for an official search of the Index Map and Parcels Index, including the list of pending applications, in respect of the land referred to below, and for a certificate of the result to be issued in the form set out below.

County, county borough
or London borough ___ BLANKSHIRE ___ Parish or place ___ NEWTOWN

Property _____ 1, MAIN STREET, NEWTOWN

_____ coloured/edged _____ on the accompanying plan
(see notes overleaf)

Signed *M. E. Purchaser.*   date 15.7.78.

OFFICIAL CERTIFICATE OF RESULT OF SEARCH

The completion of this certificate is to be effected only by H.M. Land Registry

For official use only

It is hereby certified that the official search of the Index Map applied for above has been made with the following result:

The land is not registered.

~~The land is registered freehold under Title no.~~

The land is registered leasehold under Title no. _____ held under a lease dated

and made between (1) _____

_____ Term _____ years _____ from

A rentcharge is registered under Title no. _____ created by a deed dated

and made between (1)

_____ Amount payable £

The land is not affected by any caution against first registration or by any priority notice.

~~The land is affected by a caution against first registration/priority notice registered under no.~~

~~The land is in a non-compulsory area but will be registrable on sale as from~~

The land is in a compulsory area.

OFFICIAL STAMP

HM LAND REGISTRY

N.B. Please enclose this result of search with any plan annexed with a) any correspondence b) any future first registration to which this search relates.

Fig 4

either the search 'reveals no subsisting entries', or there are a certain number of entries affecting the property as described in the attached schedule.

If entries are revealed, with the certificate of search there will be the schedule giving details of the appropriate number of local land charges which affect the property. The only kind of entry that you are likely to come across is one in respect of conditions imposed on the grant of planning permission, eg, for the construction of the property. In such cases, the vendor's answer to your preliminary enquiry 9(B)(iv) should indicate that the conditions have been complied with. If a local land charge of some other variety is revealed by the search, ask the local authority for further details.

In relation to the additional enquiries, consider the replies in conjunction with the following comments which apply equally to the two versions of the form (London, and outside London) except where a specific difference is highlighted.

1 If the answer to (A) is 'no', seek legal advice before proceeding.

2, 3 and 4 If the answer is 'yes', ask the local authority for further details.

5 The answer should be 'no'. If this is not the case, ask the local authority for further information.

6 and 7 The reply to 6(A) will normally be 'yes'. If not, seek legal advice. Where you are given an affirmative reply to enquiry 6(B), or 7, ask the local authority for more information.

8 and 9 If the answer is 'yes', ask the local authority for more information.

10 The reply should indicate that the property in which you are interested is in a residential area. If it does not, ask the local authority for further information. Also, ask the local authority for more information where the answer to part (E) (part (C) on the London councils form) is 'yes'.

11, 12 and 13 The usual reply to these enquiries, which request information in relation to development, is 'no'. If the answer is 'yes', ask the local authority for more information.

14 The answer to this enquiry will tell you whether there **are any entries on the Register of Planning Applications. The** information given in the reply should correspond with what the vendor told you in his reply to your preliminary enquiry concerning planning.

15 This enquiry concerns regulations governing the display of advertisements. It is not likely to be of much concern to you, and the reply will usually be 'no'.

16 and 17 If the answer is 'yes', ask the local authority for more information.

18, 19, 20, 21, 22 and 23 The Community Land Act 1975 gives local authorities power to acquire land which is needed for development. This group of enquiries is to discover what steps the council has taken to exercise these powers. If the answer to any of these enquiries is 'yes', ask the local authority for more information as to the effect of the reply, and, if necessary, seek legal advice before proceeding.

24 If the answer to either part of this enquiry is 'yes', ask the local authority for more information.

25 The reply to this enquiry may indicate that the property is in a smoke control area.

26 The reply may be 'yes', but this will not normally concern you provided that you intend to occupy the property immediately after completion of your purchase.

form CON 29 ENGLAND AND WALES (EXCLUDING LONDON) only

27 Where the property is in an area of compulsory registration of title, and title to the property is not already registered, you will have to apply for first registration within two months of your becoming the owner.

form CON 29 LONDON only

27, 28 and 29 The answers should be 'no'. If 'yes', ask the local authority for further information.

If you asked for any of the optional Part II enquiries to be answered and are unsure of the significance of the reply given, ask the local authority for further inormation.

The local search covers most matters within the knowledge of the local authority that are likely to concern you. However, if there is some additional point that you wish to know about, ask them.

When you have worked your way through the local search certificate and the replies to the additional enquiries, you should take the necessary action to follow through on all untoward entries. When you have done this, you must only proceed with the transaction if you are sure that you are aware of the effect and extent of the matter revealed, and are content to buy a house which is subject to that.

Remember, if you agree to buy the property, you will be agreeing to take it subject to all matters covered by your local search and enquiries. If you are not happy with what these tell you about the property, you can back out now without obligation, and you will be entitled to recover any deposit paid.

Being Sure of the Building Society Loan

If you applied to a building society for a loan they will make you a written offer if your application is successful. Read this offer very carefully. Check that all particulars, eg, the names of the borrowers, tenure of the property etc, are correct. If the offer imposes conditions which must be fulfilled before the money will be released, eg, certain works of repair, or the discharge of an existing mortgage, ask yourself whether you are in a position to comply. There is no point accepting the loan offer if you are not.

If you wish to take up the offer for a loan then sign and return the form of acceptance.

The offer of a loan is made on the understanding that the title to the property to be mortgaged is perfectly satisfactory. In due course, the building society will instruct solicitors to check this for them (at your expense!). However, there is clearly no point agreeing to buy if you know that there is something affecting the property which will prevent the loan being made. Thus, if, during your perusal of the draft contract, you came across any unusual points, eg, particularly onerous covenants, draw these to the attention of the building society and obtain their confirmation that they are prepared to accept the situation.

When you have accepted the loan offer, write to the solicitor acting for the building society and ask him to let you know what documents he will wish you to lodge with him to enable him to authorise the release of the money.

Completion Date

Before you sign the contract, you *must* be sure to agree a removal date with the vendor and insert this in the appropriate space in the contract.

A date four weeks or so after exchange of contracts will allow you sufficient time to attend to all that must be done before completion.

Exceptionally, the vendor may indicate that he is unable to agree a firm completion date at this stage, eg, because he is waiting for his new house to be built. Where this is the case, exchange of contracts will have to be delayed. You must not consider exchanging contracts unless a completion date has been agreed. If you are unhappy at the prospect of an indefinite wait, you can back out now and recover any deposit paid.

5 Agreeing to Buy

Before you formally agree to buy, you should be sure that you have attended to each of the following points.

1 You have read through the draft contract and any documents sent with it and understand their meaning and effect. Also, any necessary amendments to the draft contract have been agreed and made.

2 You have raised preliminary enquiries and have received satisfactory replies to them.

3 You have made a local search and are happy with the result.

4 You have made a land charges search and have taken the appropriate action in relation to any entries revealed.

5 You have made an index map search and understand, and agree with, the information given by the result.

6 You are sure that you can finance the transaction.

7 Where you are involved in a chain transaction (see page 147), you have read, and are prepared to follow the procedure detailed in, Chapter 14 of this book.

When you are sure that you are ready to exchange contracts, you (and any other co-purchaser) should sign your part of the draft contract. Any obvious alterations or amendments should be initialled in the margin. Insert the completion date, if this has not been done already. Do not date the contract. This will be done by the vendor's solicitor when your offer to buy is accepted.

The contract will normally require you to pay a 10 per cent deposit, and will probably stipulate that this shall be paid to the vendor's solicitor. Any sum already paid should be taken into account as part of the contract deposit.

Your part of the contract (duly signed) together with the cheque for the deposit should now be sent to the vendor's solicitor. Tell him that you look forward to receiving the vendor's part of the contract in exchange.

Where your land charges search result is to be certified by the vendor's solicitor (or he is to take some other action to satisfy you as to an entry revealed) the K18 form should be sent with the contract, and your letter should make it clear that your part of the contract is being sent on the express understanding that the appropriate certificate (or other information) will be given.

When you receive the vendor's part of the contract in exchange, check that it has been signed by the vendor, and dated, and that it contains any agreed additions or amendments.

Assuming that everything is in order, you have now agreed to buy. Congratulations, and well done!

As soon as you have exchanged contracts, you *must* insure the property. Attend to this now. In the case of leasehold property, any provisions of the lease relating to insurance, eg, stipulating the use of a particular company, must be complied with. Where you are buying the property with the aid of a mortgage, the building society's requirements regarding insurance must be adhered to.

6 Before Completion

General Considerations

Between now and completion, you will be looking at the evidence offered by the vendor in proof of his claim to own the property, and preparing the deed by which ownership will be transferred to you. A typical timetable of the various steps leading to completion is given below.

Day 1   Receive vendor's signed contract.

         Order conveyancing forms.

Day 6   Receive vendor's evidence of ownership.

Day 7   Investigate vendor's title, prepare requisitions on title and the draft purchase deed.

Day 8 Where there is a mortgage, lodge all necessary documents with the building society's solicitor and request draft mortgage.

Day 14 Receive mortgagee's solicitor's comments on title and draft mortgage.

Day 15 Submit requisitions on title, together with draft purchase deed for approval.

     Approve draft mortgage.

Day 18 Receive replies to requisitions on title and draft purchase deed approved.

Day 19 Engross and execute purchase deed.

     Send purchase deed to vendor's solicitor.

     Receive engrossed mortgage and execute same.

Day 20 Make pre-completion search.

     Receive completion statement.

Day 24 Receive result of pre-completion search.

Day 28 Completion.

In addition to attending to the above, you must also, of course, arrange your removals. If you are involved in a simultaneous sale and purchase, the removal arrangements for the two sides of the chain must be co-ordinated (see Chapter 15 of this book).

Considerable inconvenience will be caused if the completion date is not met. Further, if the delay is your own fault, the contract will normally require you to pay interest on the amount of the purchase price outstanding until completion takes place. If the delay is the vendor's fault, you will not normally have to pay that interest, but you will have no real remedy against him if he delays for only a few days. So, as the matter progresses, do all that is necessary to goad the vendor into action so that he will be ready to complete by the agreed date.

Obtaining Your Conveyancing Forms

The property that you are buying will fall into one of the following three groups in which the appropriate form requirements are detailed. The result of your index map search will enable you to identify the correct group.

(a) Title Unregistered, property NOT in an area of compulsory registration of title

    1 Oyez Publishing Ltd form CON 28B—two copies. (Order an extra copy if you are buying the property with the assistance of a mortgage.)

    2 Land Charges Act 1972 form K15—one copy.

    3 One sheet of 'Land Registry Foolscap'.

(b) Title Unregistered, property IN an area of compulsory registration of title

    1 Oyez Publishing Ltd form CON 28B—two copies. (Purchase an extra copy if you are buying the property with the aid of a mortgage.)

    2 Land Charges Act 1972 form K15—one copy.

    3 One sheet of 'Land Registry Foolscap'.

    4 One copy of HM Land Registry form 1A (or 2A where the property you are buying is leasehold).

    5 HM Land Registry form A13—three copies.

(c) Title registered

    1 Oyez Publishing Ltd form CON 28B—two copies. (Purchase an extra copy if you are buying the property with the aid of a mortgage.)

    2 Four copies of HM Land Registry form 19 (or 19(JP) where you are buying jointly with some other person). If you are buying with the aid of a mortgage, purchase one extra copy of this form.

    3 HM Land Registry form 94A—one copy.

    4 HM Land Registry form A4—one copy.

Purchase the forms you need, together with a small box of small, self-adhesive wafer seals (for use on the purchase deed).

If your vendor has agreed to assign to you the benefit of his NHBC House Purchaser's Agreement (see page 32), also obtain an assignment form, NHBC form HB12, from a branch of Oyez Stationery Ltd.

Evidence of Vendor's Ownership

What form the vendor's proof of ownership will take depends upon whether his title is registered or unregistered.

(a) Unregistered title—A vendor of land with unregistered title will supply copies of his title deeds. These copies (typed, or photographed) will be put together to form an 'abstract of title'.

(b) Registered title—Where a vendor's title to property is registered, he will supply you with a copy of the Register, and of any document referred to on it. This copy will usually be a facsimile of the Register, and will consist of perhaps two pages giving details of the three parts of the Register (A Property Register, B Proprietorship Register, C Charges Register), and a copy of the Land Registry's official plan of the propery. A specimen copy of the Register is set out on pages 64 and 65.

In addition, the vendor is also required to supply you with a signed authority to inspect the Register. This may consist of either a letter addressed to the Land Registry telling them to allow you to inspect the Register for the title concerned or, more usually, a completed printed form (form 201) to that effect.

Investigating the Vendor's Title

As you deal with this part of the procedure have pen and paper handy and make notes of any points that you consider require further clarification. Answers to these queries will be obtained by requisition on title that you will raise in due course.

As the evidence of ownership differs materially in unregistered and registered titles, we must deal with investigating title under two sections.

(a) Unregistered title—In investigating the vendor's title you will be looking through the abstract of title supplied. This sets out the history of the property, and should show an unbroken chain of ownership leading to the vendor. If it does not, you must place the matter in expert hands.

A typical abstract of title in relation to a straightforward conveyancing transaction involving freehold property, might consist of details of events as follows:

1/6/1960 CONVEYANCE—Beautiful Builders Co Ltd to John Williams Smith.

1/6/1960 MORTGAGE—John Williams Smith to Big Building Society.

10/4/1968 VACATING RECEIPT—(endorsed on mortgage dated 1/6/1960).

10/4/1968 CONVEYANCE—John Williams Smith to Albert Vendor.

10/4/1968 MORTGAGE—Albert Vendor to Bigger Building Society.

So then, to work. Read through the abstract of title considering individually each link in the chain of ownership, having particular regard to the following points.

Deeds generally

(i) *Title* A deed will usually commence with words setting out its effect, eg, 'This Conveyance'. Other kinds of deeds that you are likely to come across in the normal domestic conveyancing transaction are assignments, deeds of gift, leases, mortgages, and legal charges. If, as part of the chain of ownership, there is a document of a kind not mentioned above, eg, an indenture, assent, probate of the will or letters of administration of a deceased former owner, power of attorney, settlement, trust deed, deed of grant, deed of appointment of new trustee etc, you must seek expert assistance.

(ii) *Date* All deeds should be dated. If, according to the abstract copy, the date has been left blank, you will have to raise a requisition on title asking for confirmation that the original deed is dated. If it transpires that it is not, seek expert advice.

(iii) *Parties* Make a particular point of checking that the person disposing of property by a deed (ie, the vendor, assignor, donor or lessor) is the same person who was made the owner by the preceeding conveyance, assignment, deed of gift, or lease (as the case may be). Where there is a slight difference of spelling of the name, you must obtain the vendor's solicitor's confirmation that the two names refer to one and the same person. The name may have changed, eg, on marriage. Despite the change, that person still owns the property and can sell it, provided she supplies a copy of the marriage certificate. If two names clearly refer to different people, you must take legal advice.

Where property is transferred to joint owners, they must *all* be parties to the next deed by which ownership is passed down the line. If they are not, eg, because one of them has died in the meantime, you will need to seek expert assistance.

If someone other than the then vendor and purchaser is also a party to a conveyance, assignment, deed of gift, or a lease, eg, where a person joins in as mortgagee, or liquidator of a company, seek legal advice. Also, where a deed shows that property is being disposed of by a charity, local authority, the Church Commissioners, a trustee in bankruptcy, the Official Receiver, or some body other than a private individual or a building company, you must seek expert advice.

Following any recitals (which commence with the word 'Whereas'), the operative part of the deed (commencing with the word 'Witness(eth)') will be set out in the present tense. With modern deeds, eg, printed standard forms of mortgage, the old formula of 'Whereas' and 'Witnesseth' has given way to simple numbered clauses.

(iv) *Consideration* The first few words of the operative part of the deed usually specify the consideration, ie, the price paid. In the case of the grant of a lease, it may be that no price was paid but that the consideration was the rent reserved, and the covenants to be performed by the tenant.

There does not have to be any monetary consideration. A deed of gift is quite effective to make a person the owner of land. However, for various reasons connected with tax, where there have been two consecutive gifts of the property within the last seven years and both occurred before 27 March 1974, you must take legal advice.

(v) *Operative words* The next part of the deed is particularly important since it will state what the owner of the property is doing with it. In a conveyance, the relevant words are that the vendor(s) '*as Beneficial Owner(s)* [or *as Trustees*] hereby *convey(s)*' to the purchaser(s). An assignment of property will be effected by the same wording except that the vendor(s) will '*assign*' rather than '*convey*'. A deed of gift is effected when the owner '*as Settlor* hereby *conveys* [or *assigns*]'. In a lease, the relevant wording is that the owner 'hereby *demises*'. If a deed states that the owner is disposing of his interest in some capacity other than as beneficial owner, trustee, or settlor, you must place the matter in expert hands.

Should any of the appropriate operative words printed in italic type above have been omitted from the deed you are considering, seek legal advice.

A mortgage deed gives the lender a lease of the property for so long as there is any money outstanding, and is created by words similar to those in a lease, ie, the borrower 'hereby demises'. A legal charge (or 'charge by way of legal mortgage') gives the lender the same rights as under a mortgage when the owner states that he 'charges the property by way of legal mortgage'. In a mortgage or legal charge, you will often find that, before these words giving the lender his security, there will be a clause in which the borrower promises to pay the amount borrowed with interest.

(vi) *Description of the property* The description of the property being dealt with will either be given in full, or by reference, either to some other part of the deed, eg, a schedule, or to an earlier deed, where the full description is contained. From a reading of this full description it should be apparent that successive deeds are links in the same chain, dealing with the same property.

Where the description refers to a plan, make sure that it is complete as regards any colouring that is supposed to be on it.

The description of the land will often include the words, 'Together with the rights easements and appurtenances thereto belonging', and 'Except and Reserved all mines and minerals'. Such general expressions are quite normal and are no cause for concern. However, if some specific right, eg, a right of way, is referred to, you will have to seek expert assistance.

Your consideration of the description of the property in the deeds should ultimately show that the vendor is able to convey property matching that described in the contract. If it is apparent that he is not, seek legal advice.

(vii) *'To Hold'* Following the description, the deed will vest the property in the person in whose favour the disposition is being made. Thus, in a conveyance of freeholds there will usually be the phrase, 'To Hold the same unto the purchaser(s) *in fee simple.*' In an assignment of the benefit of a lease, the relevant wording is, 'To Hold the same unto the purchaser(s) *for the residue* now unexpired *of the term of . . . years created* [or *granted*] *by the lease*'. Where a lease is being granted, you will find the words, 'To Hold the same unto the lessee/tenant *for a term of . . . years from . . .*'. If any words other than these are used, seek legal advice. Note though, that in modern deeds you will often find that, although the main words are used (ie, those in italics above), the words 'To Hold' are omitted. In such cases the deed is perfectly effective and there is no cause for alarm.

Where you are buying leasehold property, compare the length of the term of years granted by the lease with these details as stated in the contract. If there is any discrepancy, you should seek legal advice as to your rights.

Where the deed you are considering is a mortgage, the wording will be the same as if the deed were a lease, except for the fact that it will say that the term of years granted is 'subject to a proviso for cesser on redemption'. This means that the lease granted will end when the loan is repaid. Provided that these words do appear in the deed then, if the mortgage has been discharged by a valid vacating receipt (as to which see below) or will be discharged before completion, you need not concern yourself further with the contents of the mortgage, as its provisions will have ceased to have effect. (In the case of a legal charge, no term of years is expressly granted.)

(viii) *Joint owners* Where ownership of property is being transferred to two or more persons there will probably be words indicating how they are to hold the property as between themselves, eg, 'as Trustees for sale on trust for themselves,' or 'as beneficial joint tenants'. There will probably also be a clause later in the deed, called a 'joint tenancy clause', giving further particulars of their respective rights in relation to the proceeds of sale, and their powers to mortgage, charge, or lease the property.

(ix) *Subject to . . .* In the case of freehold land, the conveyance or deed of gift may state that the property is 'Subject to the restrictive and other covenants and conditions and the agreements and declarations hereinafter contained'. The reference may be to such matters as they are detailed in some other deed. In either case, you must be sure that you know what matters the property is subject to and their effect.

If you now find that the property is subject to something that you were not told about before you agreed to buy, the vendor is in breach of his obligations, and you should seek legal advice.

An assignment or deed of gift of leasehold property will normally state that the term of years transferred is 'subject to the payment of the yearly rent of . . . reserved by the lease and to the performance and observance of the covenants on the part of the lessee and the conditions therein contained'.

A lease will include the words 'Yielding and Paying therefor during the said term the yearly rent of . . . by equal [half-]yearly payments on the . . . day of . . . [and the . . . day of . . .] in each year'.

(x) *Other clauses* You may find that covenants, ie, promises, are included as part of the deed. For example, a buyer may agree to erect a fence round the property, or may agree not to use the property as anything other than a private dwelling-house. In all probability, so far as any such covenants will affect you, their existence will have been brought to your attention before you agreed to buy. If this was not the case, seek legal advice.

When an owner of property which is affected by covenants sells his land, he often requires the purchaser to promise to observe the covenants in future and to indemnify him from liability for their breach.

At the end of the deed you are quite likely to come across a 'certificate of value' clause which declares that the value of the transaction does not exceed a certain figure. The significance of this clause is explained later under the heading 'Stamp duties'.

(xi) *Acknowledgement and undertaking* On completion of a sale, the vendor will normally hand to the purchaser all the original title deeds and documents as detailed in the abstract of title. Where he is selling only part of what he owns, he will not wish to do this since it would leave him nothing with which to prove that he is the owner of what he retains. But the purchaser needs to be given the right to use those previous deeds to prove his ownership of what he is now buying. This right will be given to him by an 'acknowledgement and undertaking' clause which states that the vendor acknowledges the purchaser's right to production of the prior title deeds (detailing those concerned) and undertakes to keep them safe. (Where vendors sell as trustees, they give the acknowledgement only and not the undertaking.)

Where the deed that you are examining disposes of only part of property, be sure that it contains the appropriate acknowledgement and undertaking for previous deeds. If it does not, seek expert assistance.

Where part of leasehold property has been sold off, you will often find that it was agreed that, from then on, the rent would be split between the two properties. In such cases, the sale deed will contain promises by the respective parties that they will each pay their own part of the rent and will indemnify the other from claims in respect of it.

So far as any remaining clauses are concerned, read through them to see what matters affect the property. If you are in any doubt as to the effect of a particular clause, you will have to take legal advice.

(xii) *Execution* To be effective, a deed must be signed, sealed and delivered by the person making the disposition.

In typed abstracts of title, the fact that a deed has been executed will be indicated by the words 'Signed, sealed, and delivered' (or the abbreviation, 'SSD') followed by the name of the person executing the document. To show that the deed was executed in the presence of a witness the abstract may include the words, '. . . and attested'.

If your abstract consists of photocopies, you will be able to see the words 'Signed, sealed and delivered by the said . . .' with the signature of that person alongside.

Proper execution of a deed includes sealing. Where you have a photocopy of the deed, it should show the seal. In the case of typed copies, the letters 'LS' will be put to indicate where the seal appears on the original.

A company executes a deed by the affixing of the company seal in the presence of a director and the company secretary, clerk, or other permanent officer, or his deputy. These two witnesses to the sealing of the deed will add their signatures by way of attestation.

In cases where a deed appears to have been executed by a person as attorney (ie, agent) of the person who is the party to the deed, and not by that party personally, take legal advice.

Should the abstract not give the appropriate indication of due execution, you must raise a requisition on title asking the vendor's solicitor to confirm that the deed has been properly executed. If a deed has not been properly executed, seek expert assistance.

(xiii) *Stamp duties* Governments levy a tax, 'stamp duty', on documents giving effect to certain transactions. Duty is payable on a deed conveying the ownership of property, whether that deed is a conveyance, assignment, transfer, or deed of gift, and also on a deed granting a lease.

You must satisfy yourself that each and every deed in the title to the property that you have agreed to buy (other than mortgages and legal charges) has been properly stamped.

In a typed abstract, details of the stamping will be given at the start of the deed in the left-hand margin alongside the date, eg, '£28'. Where the abstract consists of photocopies, you will be able to see details of the stamping at the top of the front page.

The rates of stamp duty are as given below.

(a) *Stamp duty on a deed conveying ownership* To work out the amount of duty that should have been paid, first ascertain the date of the deed concerned. Then find out the price paid for the property at that time. (Where no price was paid, ie, the deed is a voluntary conveyance, a deed of gift, see below as to the stamp duty situation.)

It was, and still is, possible, in appropriate cases, to obtain reliefs in the form of exemptions and reduced rates of duty if the deed contains a certificate of value at certain figures. If a deed contains such a clause, note the amount of the certificate.

Applying whichever one of Tables 1–11 on pages 155–64 is appropriate having regard to the date of the deed, you should now check that the stamp duty that was paid in respect of each link in the chain of ownership was correct.

To take an example, to calculate the stamp duty which should have been paid on a conveyance dated 10 April 1968, with a price of £5,600 and a certificate of value in the sum of £7,000, one must apply Table 8 on page 161. The consideration of the deed falls within the limits of the next but last column down, and the certificate of value will mean that the appropriate rate of duty was '5s 0d, for every £50 or part thereof'. On a price of £5,600 this works out at £28.

If the stamping on a deed is incorrect, you must raise a requisition on title asking the vendor's solicitor to explain the discrepancy.

Quite apart from the question of stamping in respect of any duty payable, every conveyance, assignment, or transfer of property dated on or after 1 September 1931 should be stamped to show that it has been produced to the Inland Revenue and certain particulars given. In a typed abstract, this will be indicated by the marking 'P' or 'PD', or 'produced' in the left-hand margin. If a deed you are considering requires the produced stamp and it does not appear to have one, this must be made the subject of a requisition on title.

If no price was paid, the deed must have been delivered to the Inland Revenue for them to adjudicate the real value of the property transferred. When this was done, the deed would then have been stamped 'adjudicated' and any duty would have been paid, and stamps impressed. So, where you are considering a deed of gift, this is what you should be looking for.

(b) *Stamp duty on a lease* In relation to a lease, stamp duty is payable by reference to the rent reserved, and any premium, ie, price paid. It is possible to obtain reliefs in the form of duty at reduced rates where the lease contains a certificate of value in respect of the consideration involved (other than rent). If the lease you are considering is so certified, note at what amount.

Having regard to the date of the lease, you can calculate the stamp duty that should have been paid by applying whichever one of tables A–E on pages 165–9 is appropriate. Each table includes two calculations. The first is to determine the duty in respect of the rent reserved by the lease, and the second is to determine the duty in respect of the price paid (if any).

If the lease on the title of the property you are buying does not appear to have been properly stamped, you will have to raise a requisition on title asking the vendor's solicitor for an explanation.

Also, whether or not the lease requires stamping in respect of any duty payable, if it is dated on or after 1 September 1931 it must bear a 'produced' stamp to show that it was delivered to the Inland Revenue and certain particulars given. In relation to this 'produced' stamp, see the comments above.

Root of title The abstract of title must commence with the deed specified in the contract as the root of title. You are not entitled to go back beyond the root of title, except that if a deed refers to, eg, a plan, or covenants etc, in an earlier deed, you should be given a copy of that material.

Mortgages Once you have decided that a particular deed is a mortgage or legal charge, your only concern is to be sure that it has been discharged.

A mortgage or legal charge is discharged by a vacating receipt, which you will usually find endorsed on the back of the mortgage deed. This will state that, on a particular date, the lender acknowledged that he had received a certain sum representing the balance of monies due to him under the mortgage, together with all interest and costs, payment having been made by a particular person. To be effective the vacating receipt must have been signed by the lender. If the receipt shows that someone other than the original borrower made repayment, seek legal advice.

A receipt by a building society will simply state that they have received all monies intended to be secured by the mortgage (without mentioning any amount, or the person making repayment). Such a receipt is effective to end the mortgage if the seal of the society was affixed in the presence of a person authorised for that purpose by the board of directors or committee of management.

Searches The abstract of title will probably contain details of the land charges searches made immediately before each disposition of the property. If it does not, ask the vendor's solicitor for such information. Check that before each transfer of ownership a search was made against the name of the person who was then the vendor. Should it be that a search was not made then, look to see if that name was included in a later search. A search should have been made against the names of all owners of the land as detailed in the abstract of title (or since 1/1/26, if the chain of ownership stretches back that far). If some names do not appear to have had the necessary search made against them and those names were not included in your pre-contract search, make a note to make a search yourself before completion (see page 84).

In relation to each search made, note the result and consider any entries revealed by it in conjunction with the comments on pages 36–40. Normally, the only entries that you will be prepared to take the property subject to are those of class D(ii), ie, relating to restrictive covenants. Where the search shows that, at the time it was made, the property was subject to, eg, a registration of class C(i), C(iii), or F, the vendor's solicitor must supply evidence to show that the registration has been, or will be cancelled.

The abstract will give the date on which the search was made. To protect a purchaser against entries put on the register after that date and before he completes his purchase, a certificate of result of search gives a certain period of protection. Prior to the 25 November 1940, this period of protection was two working days; from that date until 1 March 1972 it was fourteen working days, and on that date it was increased to fifteen working days. If the transaction was completed outside the period of protection afforded by the search result, you cannot rely on its results so far as a search against the person who then owned the property is concerned. You will have to make a further search against that name before completion.

Additionally, where a former owner of the property happened to be a company, a search should have been made in a separate register maintained especially for companies. The abstract should give details of this 'company search'. If it does not, cover the point by a requisition on title. If the vendor's solicitor states that no such search was made, place the matter in expert hands.

The result of a company search will usually consist of a letter from a firm of law agents stating that they have made a search of the Register. Normally, there will be no adverse entries. eg, proposals for winding up, that might affect a buyer. However, a type of entry that is met not infrequently is a floating charge. Here, a buyer requires some evidence of non-crystalisation. This is usually given by a letter to that effect from the person entitled to the benefit of the charge. If the company search revealed such an entry and no such letter was obtained, seek expert assistance.

(b) Registered title—In this part of the procedure you will be looking at the copy of the Register for the vendor's title to see what he is able to transfer. (A specimen set of Land Registry entries are set out on pages 64 and 65.)

At the top of the front page will be details of when the Register was opened, the title number (check that this agrees with the information in the contract and on the index map search), and the number of pages to the Register (make sure that your copy contains all the pages in addition to the plan of the property).

The body of the Register is in three parts.

Part A: Property Register describes the property, and contains details of any rights benefiting it. The description will refer to the plan filed at the Registry. Be sure that a copy of this plan has been supplied to you. Check that it correctly represents what the vendor has agreed to sell. If there is any discrepancy between the extent of the property that you have personally inspected, what the vendor contracted to sell, and what the Register says he owns, seek legal advice. Also, where the vendor agreed to sell the property with the benefit of some particular right, eg, a right of way, make sure that this is mentioned in this part of the Register.

H.M. LAND REGISTRY

Edition 1   opened 20.5.1968   TITLE NUMBER BA123456   *This register consists of* 2

A. PROPERTY REGISTER
containing the description of the registered land and the estate comprised in the Title

COUNTY	DISTRICT
BLANKSHIRE	NEWTOWN

The Freehold land shown and edged with red on the plan of the above Title filed at the Registry
registered on 20 May 1968 known as 1 Main Street.

(no particular rights benefitting the property)

SPECIMEN

B. PROPRIETORSHIP REGISTER
stating nature of the Title, name, address and description of the proprietor of the land and any entries affecting the right of disposing thereof

TITLE ABSOLUTE

Entry number	Proprietor, etc.	Remarks
1.	ALBERT VENDOR of 1 Main Street, Newtown, Blankshire, Plumber, registered on 20 May 1968.	Price paid £5600
	(no restriction affecting the proprietor)	

SPECIMEN

Any entries struck through are no longer subsisting

Demand No. 535692 105,000 24.2.77 W.G. & F.M. Ltd.

TITLE NUMBER BA123456

C. CHARGES REGISTER

containing charges, incumbrances etc., adversely affecting the land and registered dealings therewith

Entry Number	The date at the beginning of each entry is the date on which the entry was made on this edition of the register	Remarks
1.	20 May 1968 - A Conveyance of the land in this title dated 1 June 1960 made between (1) Beautiful Builders Company Limited (Company) and (2) John William Smith (Purchaser) contains the following covenant:- "The Purchaser hereby covenants with the Company for the benefit of the Company's adjoining land known as 2 to 10 (even) Main Street that no building erected on the land hereby conveyed shall be used other than as a private dwellinghouse."	
2.	20 May 1968 - CHARGE dated 10 April 1968 registered on 20 May 1968 to secure the moneys therein mentioned.	
3.	PROPRIETOR - BIGGER BUILDING SOCIETY of 47 Church Street, Blanktown, Blankshire, registered on 20 May 1968.	

SPECIMEN

Any entries struck through are no longer subsisting

Fig 5

In detailing the rights that benefit the property, the Property Register may refer to some deed where such matters are set out in full. If this is the case, be sure that you have been given a copy of such document and that you have read and understood the same.

The description of the property will also state whether the registered title is freehold or leasehold. This information should correspond with what the vendor has agreed to sell.

Where the property is leasehold, the Property Register will give details of the lease (date, parties, term granted etc). Compare the details there set out with those stated in the contract. Where they do not agree, take legal advice. At this point in the case of leasehold property, you should read the lease, if you have not done so already. All the covenants given by the original lessee/ tenant in his capacity as such will be binding on you when you take over the lease. In rare cases, the lease may originally have been granted in respect of the piece of land that you are buying and also some other piece of land which is now owned separately. Where this has happened, the Property Register will probably indicate that, at the time of the split, it was agreed that the rent reserved by the lease should be apportioned between the respective properties.

Part B: Proprietorship Register will, first of all, give details of the quality of title awarded in respect of the registered interest, eg, absolute, or good leasehold, depending upon what the vendor agreed to sell. If the copy entries indicate that the vendor merely has qualified, or possessory title, you must take legal advice.

Below the description of the quality of the title will be details of the registered proprietor(s). Former proprietors will have had their names ruled out. The Register should show that the vendor(s) (as described in the contract) is (are) the proprietor(s). If it does not, then, subject to the following comments, take legal advice. The two situations where this will not be necessary are as follows. First, you can safely proceed where the registered proprietor is a woman whose name has changed by marriage after she became owner. In such cases, all you need is an official copy of the marriage certificate. Second, where the person now selling is only one of the persons specified on the Register as being joint registered proprietors, he may have the power to sell if all the others have died (see next paragraph), when all you need is an official copy of the death certificate(s).

Where the property is jointly owned, there may be a restriction set out in the Proprietorship Register stating that no disposition by one of the proprietors (as survivor, where the others have died) can be registered except by order of the Registrar or the court. Such a restriction is of no concern to you provided that all the proprietors mentioned on the Register are now selling. If there are more than two proprietors detailed on the Register then, provided that at least two of them are now alive, those survivors can validly sell the property to you even where the restriction mentioned above does appear on the Register. Where there is no such restriction on the Register, the sole living survivor of any number of joint owners can sell.

In the remarks column alongside the name of the proprietor, there may be details of the price paid by him.

Where a husband or wife is alone registered as proprietor, the Proprietorship Register may contain an entry called a 'caution under the Matrimonial Homes Act 1967' which protects the right of a non-owning spouse to occupy the matrimonial home. If such an entry appears on the Register that you are examining, raise a requisition on title stipulating that, on completion, a signed form of application for cancellation of the caution entry (form 71) must be handed over.

The Proprietorship Register may also state that certain promises have previously been made by the registered proprietor, eg, that he would erect a fence, or discharge some other positive obligation. Normally, such positive covenants will not concern you unless, in the contract, you agreed that you would covenant to perform the obligation concerned and indemnify the vendor from future liability.

Should it be that there is an entry on the Proprietorship Register of a kind not referred to above, eg, a caution against dealing with the property in some particular way, or an entry referring to the bankruptcy of the registered proprietor, requiring the proprietor to obtain the consent of certain persons before disposing of his interest, or mentioning the Settled Land Act 1925, seek expert assistance.

Part C: Charges Register contains details of all charges and incumbrances affecting the registered title.

Where the property is subject to the burden of some restrictive covenant or a right in favour of a third party granted by a deed, eg, a right of way, the Charges Register will usually contain full details of the matter concerned. Occasionally, such details may be given by referring you to the document where the matter is set out in full. Be sure that you have been supplied with a copy of the relevant document, and have read and understood the same. You should have been told before you agreed to buy that the property is affected by such incumbrances.

If the property is subject to a charge, ie, a mortgage, you will require confirmation that, on completion, you will be given a completed form of discharge.

The rights of occupation of a non-owning spouse may be protected by an entry on Part B of the Register or by an entry on this part of the Register. To secure the removal of such an entry on the Charges Register, it is sufficient if the non-owning spouse signs a letter releasing his/her rights. That letter must be handed over on completion.

If there are any entries on the Charges Register of a kind other than those described above, eg, referring to leases, or death duties, take legal advice before proceeding.

Requisitions on Title

If, in the course of your investigation of the vendor's title, you came across points of difficulty, these will be resolved by 'requisitions on title'. At this stage you will also put other questions to the vendor on certain more general matters.

You will be completing Oyez Publishing Ltd's form CON 28B, in duplicate (or in triplicate where you are buying with the aid of a mortgage). The form should be headed in the same way as your preliminary enquiries. As to completion of the remainder of the form, note the following comments.

3 Title deeds Where title is unregistered, delete part (B). Where title is registered, delete part (A) and part (B) questions (ii) and (iii).

4 Mortgages If the property is subject to a subsisting mortgage, strictly speaking, it should be discharged before completion, and at that time you should be given the appropriate evidence of repayment. In the case of unregistered land this consists of a vacating receipt endorsed on the mortagge deed; with registered title, a separate form of discharge, form 53.

Because the vendor is usually hoping to pay off his mortgage with the money that he will receive on completion, the practice has developed in the legal profession whereby the purchaser's solicitor, on completion, accepts the vendor's solicitor's undertaking to pay off the mortgage out of the purchase moneys and to forward the vacating receipt (or discharge form) as soon as it is to hand. This practice could cause a purchaser considerable difficulty. You must have nothing to do with such undertakings, but rather you must insist on your strict legal rights and demand that, on completion, you must be given the completed vacating receipt (or form of discharge).

Having regard to the above comments, it will be necessary to amend part (B) of the requisition. In (i) delete 'will' in line one, and in line three, put the mark ' ʎ ' between the words 'dealing' and 'be', and write in the margin 'must'. Delete the question mark at the end of the requisition, and B(ii).

6 Possession Since you are buying the property with vacant possession, part (B) should be deleted.

Where you are buying property with registered title and the Register referred you to a deed, eg, the lease in the case of leasehold property, in which covenants or rights burdening or benefiting the property were set out in full, you must raise a requisition asking for confirmation that the original deed (or an acknowledgement and undertaking for it—see page 57) will be handed over on completion.

This further requisition should be written in the space remaining on the last page along with any other requisitions necessary to cover any specific problems you encountered in investigating

title (continuing on a separate sheet as necessary). Such additional requisitions could deal with, eg, entries on land charges
searches, removal of registrations protecting a spouse's right
of occupation, and copy marriage certificates, etc.

Drafting the Purchase Deed

You must now prepare the draft of the document by which
ownership of the property will be transferred to you. Ultimately,
the draft purchase deed will be typed, but, before you reach that
stage, you should make notes of the clauses which must be
included and write out a rough, long-hand copy.

To prepare the draft purchase deed, apply one of the following two sections, depending upon whether you are buying
property with unregistered or registered title.

(a) Unregistered—You will find a specimen form of purchase
deed set out in Fig 6 on pages 72 and 73. The preparation of
your draft purchase deed will consist of copying out this specimen, completing the blank spaces as you proceed.

We will first of all consider the preparation of the draft purchase deed as this should be done in the case of freehold property.

You should head the document as indicated, but leave the date
blank.

In the space provided for details of the vendor, enter the *full*
names of *all* the present owners of the property, and their address
(and occupation(s). if you know this). The names should correspond precisely with the details of those persons as given in
the previous deed when the property was transferred to them.
If there has been a change of name (eg, on marriage) refer to
the present and former names. Alongside the heading 'The
Purchaser' insert the *full* name of yourself and any other
person(s) who is/are to be joint owners with you (not to exceed,
in total, four in number) and their addresses and occupations.

The purpose of clause one is to give a description sufficient
to enable the property to be identified. In most cases, the deed
which gave ownership to the vendor will have contained a full
description of the property or, if it did not, it will have referred

to another deed which did describe the property fully. Since you are now probably buying all that was transferred to him, all you need do is to describe the property briefly (postal address will usually suffice) and refer to it as being, eg, 'the property comprised in and more particularly described by' that earlier conveyance (giving the date, and parties).

If the description in the previous deed does not accurately describe what the vendor has now agreed to sell, refer back to it, but point out how the description differs from what you are buying.

In framing a suitable description of the property, you will probably find that the one given in the contract is a very useful guide.

The price should be inserted, in words and figures, in clause two.

To complete clause three, look at the contract to see how the vendor is to convey, ie, whether as beneficial owner, or trustees.

The whole of clause four should be included in your draft as set out in the specimen. There is no need to make any alteration to the clause (eg, by removing (a) or (e) where you are buying on your own from a sole vendor) since it is worded in such a way that its provisions will only apply where they are relevant.

Part (e) of the clause provides that joint purchasers will be joint tenants beneficially. This means that if one of them dies his share will automatically pass to the survivor(s). It is presumed that, if you are one of joint purchasers, you and your co-purchaser are husband and wife. A husband and wife usually hold property as beneficial joint tenants. If you do not wish to, take legal advice.

Whether or not clause five, the certificate of value, should be included will depend upon the price you have agreed to pay, and whether or not the transfer of this property is only part of a larger transaction between you and the vendor. If the price you are paying for this property (and any other property which is part of the same transaction with the vendor) exceeds £30,000, this clause should be omitted. Otherwise, the clause should be included and completed by inserting at the end the lowest

THIS CONVEYANCE is dated

and is made between the VENDOR:

and the PURCHASER:

1   The Property is

2   The Price (receipt of which the Vendor acknowledges) is

                                              (£   ).

3   In consideration of the Price the Vendor as
    hereby conveys the Property to the Purchaser in fee simple.

4   The provisions of this clause shall have effect only to the extent
    that they are relevant and not inconsistent with any other
    provision of this document:

    (a) Singular includes plural and vice versa:

    (b) Covenants are joint and several if made by more than one
         person;

    (c) The property is conveyed with the benefit of all subsisting
         rights but subject as appears in any document referred to in
         Clause 1 above;

    (d) The Purchaser covenants with the Vendor by way of indemnity
         only to observe and perform any covenant stipulation or
         provision subject to which the Property is conveyed for
         breach or non-performance of which the Vendor will or may
         remain liable (either directly or by way of indemnity) after
         this disposition and to indemnify the Vendor against
         liability arising from future breach or non-performance of
         the same;

    (e) If the Purchaser is more than one person then the persons
         constituting the Purchaser declare that they are beneficial

joint tenants and that the trustees for sale for the time being of this deed shall have all the powers of an absolute owner.

5   It is hereby certified that the transaction hereby effected does not form part of a larger transaction or of a series of transactions in respect of which the amount or value or the aggregate amount or value of the consideration exceeds £

IN WITNESS whereof the parties have hereunto set their hands and seals the day and year first before written.

SIGNED SEALED AND DELIVERED)
)
by the said   )
)
in the presence of   )

SIGNED SEALED AND DELIVERED)
)
by the said   )
)
in the presence of   )

Fig 6

possible of the amounts £15,000, £20,000, £25,000 or £30,000 having regard to the price. This will enable you to obtain the best possible rebate in respect of the stamp duty.

At the foot of the deed include a sufficient number of attestation clauses ('Signed, sealed and delivered . . .') for each individual who is a party to the deed. Put that person's name in the space in each clause.

If the tenure of the property you are buying is leasehold, the instructions given above should be amended as follows.

Alter the heading from 'This Conveyance . . .' to 'This Assignment . . .'.

In describing the property in the first clause, you must refer to the lease (or underlease) which granted the term of years that you are now buying. Where you are buying only part of the property leased by that deed, refer to the later assignment where the part you are now buying is accurately described and refer to it as being 'part of the property comprised in a Lease date . . .' etc.

In clause three, change the words 'hereby conveys' to 'hereby assigns', and, at the end, put 'for the residue of the term of years granted by the Lease referred to in clause 1 above', instead of 'in fee simple'.

From your rough long-hand copy, type the draft purchase deed in duplicate on plain white paper. Where you are buying with the aid of a mortgage take an extra carbon copy.

(b) Where the vendor's title is registered—Preparing the draft purchase deed consists of completing Land Registry form 19, Transfer of Whole, (or 19(JP), where you are buying jointly with another person).

In the heading, put the county and district, the title number, and the address of the property, as this information appears in the copy of the Land Registry entries supplied to you. Leave the date blank.

Following the words 'In consideration of . . .', insert, in words and figures, the price that you have agreed to pay for the property. Do not delete the words *'the receipt whereof is hereby acknowledged'* at the end of that section.

Next, after the introduction 'I', enter, in *block letters,* the *full* name, address, and the occupation of the present owner of the property. If there is more than one person registered as proprietor, substitute 'We' for 'I'. These details of the vendor(s) should correspond precisely with the details of the registered proprietor(s) as set out on the Register, except where, eg, one or more of those registered proprietors has died, or a name has changed, eg, on marriage.

The form continues, *'as beneficial owner(s)* hereby transfer to :'. The words in italics should be made to agree with those in the contract which specify the capacity in which the vendor will convey (ie, beneficial owner(s), or trustees).

In the box enter, in *block letters,* the *full* name, address and occupation of yourself and any other person who is to be a joint owner of the property with you (not to exceed four in number).

The space before the certificate of value clause is to allow for the inclusion of any extra clauses as required by the purchase contract. If any additional clause(s) will be too long to fit into the space allowed, type in as much as you can, and then continue on the back. Where you have had to continue over in this way, all the printed clauses that you have had to jump must be ruled out and typed in the space remaining on the reverse side of the form immediately following the end of the extra clause(s).

If the property you are dealing with is freehold, the following clause must be added to the transfer form where the property is subject to some covenant or stipulation :

> The transferee [or, 'transferees jointly and severally' if you are buying jointly with some other person] covenant(s) with the transferor by way of indemnity only to observe and perform any covenant or stipulation referred to in the Charges Register of the title above mentioned for breach or non-performance of which the transferor will remain liable (either directly or by way of indemnity) after this transfer and to indemnify the transferor against all liability arising from future breach or non-performance of the same.

On form 19(JP), before the certificate of value clause, the purchasers declare whether they are to be joint tenants or tenants

Stamp pursuant to section 28 of the Finance Act, 1931, to be impressed here.	When the transfer attracts Inland Revenue duty, the stamps should be impressed here before lodging the transfer for registration

(1) For a transfer by a company or corporation form 19(Co) is printed and for a transfer to joint proprietors form 19(JP) is printed.

(1) TRANSFER OF WHOLE (Freehold or Leasehold)

(Rule 98 or 115, Land Registration Rules, 1925)

County and district (or London borough) } BLANKSHIRE, NEWTOWN.

Title number .... BA 123456

Property .... 1, MAIN STREET, NEWTOWN, BLANKSHIRE.

Date .... 19 78 . In consideration of .Eleven thousand five hundred ————

(2) Strike out if not required.

(3) In BLOCK LETTERS, enter full name(s), postal address(es) and occupation(s) of the proprietor(s) of the land.

———— pounds (£ 11,500 ————) (2)the receipt whereof is hereby acknowledged

I, (3) ALBERT VENDOR OF 1 MAIN STREET NEWTOWN BLANKSHIRE
PLUMBER

(4) If desired or otherwise as the case may be (See rules 76 and 77).

(5) In BLOCK LETTERS, enter full name, postal address and occupation of the transferee for entry on the register.

(4)as beneficial owner hereby transfer to:

(5) MARTIN EDWARD PURCHASER OF THE PIER HOTEL WIGAN LANCASHIRE
TEACHER

(6) If there is not sufficient room for any special clauses they should be continued over the page; the execution and attestation should then be added at the end.

(7) A transfer for charitable uses should follow form 36 in the schedule to the Land Registration Rules, 1925 (see rules 121 and 122).

(8) If a certificate of value for the purposes of the Stamp Act, 1891, and amending Acts is not required, this paragraph should be deleted.

the land comprised in the title above mentioned (6) (7)

The transferee covenants with the transferor by way of indemnity only to observe and perform any covenant or stipulation referred

It is hereby certified that the transaction hereby effected does not form part of a larger transaction or series of transactions in respect of which the amount or value or aggregate amount or value of the consideration exceeds £......................

Signed, sealed and delivered by the said }

.... } ....

Seal

in the presence of

Name ....

Address ....

Occupation ....

Printed in England by The Ludo Press Ltd., London SW18 3DG and published by Her Majesty's Stationery Office
1½p net or 25 for 31p net (exclusive of tax)
Dd 502847 K200 12/74
ISBN 0 11 390034 1

to in the Charges Register of the title above mentioned for
breach or non-performance of which the transferor will remain
liable (either directly or by way of indemnity) after this
transfer and to indemnify the transferor against all liability
arising from future breach or non-performance of the same.

It is hereby certified that the transaction hereby effected
does not form part of a larger transaction or series of transactions in respect of which the amount or value or the aggregate amount or value of the consideration exceeds £15,000.

SIGNED SEALED AND DELIVERED)
by the said ALBERT VENDOR)
in the presence of)

SIGNED SEALED AND DELIVERED)
by the said MARTIN EDWARD)
PURCHASER in the presence of)

Fig 7

in common of the property, ie, whether or not, on death, the deceased's share in the property is to pass to the survivor. In the normal case, a husband and wife will hold property as joint tenants. To achieve this effect, in this clause of the transfer, delete the word 'cannot'.

The final clause, the certificate of value, is to enable you to obtain relief in respect of government tax, stamp duty, payable on the transfer. If the price you are paying for the property exceeds £30,000, no relief can be claimed so the clause should be deleted. If you are able to certify that the transfer does not form part of a transaction or series of transactions with the vendor in respect of which the price or total price does not exceed £30,000, then the clause should be allowed to remain. It is completed by inserting at the end the lowest possible of the amounts £15,000, £20,000, £25,000 or £30,000, depending upon the price you are paying.

To conclude, provide attestation clauses (ie, Signed, sealed and delivered etc . . .') sufficient for all concerned. On form 19, only one attestation clause is printed, so at least one more should be added (for the purchaser). On form 19(JP), three are printed which may, or may not, be sufficient for your purposes. If you are short of space, there is no objection to referring to more than one person, eg, a husband and wife, in the same attestation clause.

An example of what a completed form 19 might look like is given in Fig 7 on pages 76 and 77.

When you have done your rough draft and are sure that it is correct, you should complete the form of transfer, in duplicate, by typing in the additions. Where you are buying the property with the aid of a mortgage, prepare one extra copy for the lender's solicitor.

Dealing with the Building Society's Solicitor

If you are not buying with the assistance of a mortgage, this part of the book will be of no concern to you. Proceed to the next section, 'Submitting Requisitions on Title and Draft Purchase Deed for Approval'. (It gets more like monopoly every minute!)

Where you are going to mortgage the property to raise part of the purchase money you must now lodge with the building society's solicitor the complete abstract of title (or office copy entries), your proposed requisitions on title and draft purchase deed, and your local search. Send the two carbon copies of both the requisitions and the draft purchase deed. Ask the solicitor to consider these with a view to approving, amending, or adding to them. One carbon copy of each will be returned to you in due course. Incorporate any required additions or alterations suggested by the building society's solicitor in the top copy of each document that you retained in your file.

With the letter returning your requisitions on title and the draft purchase deed, or perhaps a few days later, you will receive the draft mortgage deed for approval. You must check this through to see that it is correct, and to discover the extent of your obligations under it.

In most cases, the draft mortgage will consist of a printed form with the blanks completed as appropriate. Make sure that the names, amount of loan and repayments, and the description of the property are correct. Any errors or omissions should be corrected (preferably in red).

Read through the printed clauses of the mortgage deed. You may find that some of them are incomprehensible to you. Often, building societies produce a booklet explaining their mortgage clauses and, if you have been provided with such by the building society's solicitor, you will find it most helpful.

Besides containing promises by you to repay the loan with interest, the mortgage will usually provide that you cannot lease or let the property without consent, and will probably contain clauses dealing with insurance of the property and the effect of default on your part. If you are in any doubt as to the effect of any of the printed clauses, telephone the building society's solicitor. He will be able to explain matters to you. The terms of the printed mortgage forms used by the major building societies are perfectly reasonable. If you cannot obtain the necessary explanation of the meaning of the form, or you are dealing with a form of mortgage other than a standard form issued by a building society, you should seek legal advice.

When you have approved the mortgage, return it (retaining the carbon copy which will have accompanied it) to the building society's solicitor. Ask him to forward the engrossment of the mortgage deed as soon as possible, together with a statement of the precise amount of money that will be available to you on completion.

Submitting Requisitions on Title and Draft Purchase Deed for Approval

Now that the requisitions on title and draft purchase deed have been prepared (and, if there is a building society involved, have been approved by their solicitor) they can be sent, in duplicate, to the vendor's solicitor.

Replies to Requisitions on Title

All the replies to the requisitions should be clear and concise. Any that are vague or otherwise inconclusive should be referred back to the vendor's solicitor. The replies that you can expect to receive to your requisitions on form CON 28B are considered below.

1 Previous enquiries The answer will usually be in the affirmative. Any variations in preliminary enquiry replies should be satisfactorily explained.

2 Receipts Again, the answer should be in the affirmative. There should be nothing in the reply to part B(ii) which would indicate that covenants have been broken. If such appears to be the case, seek legal advice.

3 Title deeds If title to the property is not registered, the answer to A(i) will either indicate that the originals of all abstracted documents are to be handed over on completion, or that only certain ones will be given to you.

For any deeds that are not to be handed over, your investigation of title should have revealed an acknowledgement and undertaking.

In the case of property with registered title, in reply to part B(i), you will be given a particular date. This date may be relevant later in connection with your pre-completion search.

4 Mortgages The answer to both parts A and B(i) should be 'agreed', or words to that effect. No other answer will suffice. You must not accept an undertaking to discharge the mortgage out of the proceeds of sale after completion.

5 Completion Completion usually takes place at the offices of the solicitor acting for the vendor, or the vendor's building society.

The answer to part B may be 'herewith', or 'to follow'. If a completion statement is enclosed, no action is required at the moment.

On completion you will have to pay the purchase price by means of a banker's draft. If the vendor is proposing to use part of the proceeds of sale on completion to pay off his mortgage, he may well want the proceeds of sale split between his solicitor and his building society. The answer to part C will detail his requirements.

6 Possession The answer to A(i) can only be 'agreed', or words to that effect. As to arrangements for delivery of the keys of the property, whatever the vendor suggests should be consistent with his obligation to give vacant possession once the price is paid.

7 Notices In the case of freehold property, it is unlikely that any person will have to be given notice of the change of ownership.

If you are in any doubt about the answer to any of the requisitions on title, whether one of the standard printed questions or one of the specific ones you raised to cover some apparent problem with the title, refer it back to the vendor's solicitor in writing. If his reply seems to be inconclusive and the problem cannot be resolved by further discussion with him, seek legal advice.

Where you are buying the property with the aid of a mortgage, any untoward replies to requisitions must be referred to the building society's solicitor.

Approval of the Draft Purchase Deed

With his replies to your requisitions on title, the vendor's solicitor will probably return your draft of the purchase deed approved, either 'as drawn', or with any amendments necessary to make it accord with the terms of the contract.

Where amendments have been made, check that they are, in fact, correct, referring to the abstract of title as necessary.

If you are buying the property with the aid of a mortgage, any substantial amendments made by the vendor's solicitor to your draft of the purchase deed should be communicated to the building society solicitor for his approval.

When the draft has been approved by all concerned, the 'engrossment' of it can be prepared.

Engrossing the Purchase Deed

'Engrossing the purchase deed' is typing the formal document which, in due course, will be executed by the vendor and yourself.

Where title to the property is unregistered, the deed will be typed on 'Land Registry foolscap'. If the property is in an area of compulsory registration of title, take a carbon copy of the engrossment, but not otherwise.

If title is already registered, you will be typing a further copy of Land Registry form 19, or 19(JP). Take a carbon copy as you type the engrossment.

Where you are typing on Land Registry foolscap, continue on the inside pages if necessary. Leave a good margin along the fold (about $1\frac{1}{4}$in will suffice) so that the document could be stitched into a Land Registry Land Certificate should this ever be necessary. On Land Registry form 19, follow the established margins. Do not leave more than the normal line space between the end of one clause and the start of the next. If there are any such spaces left in the form 19, they must be ruled through.

Affix one adhesive red wafer seal for each person who is

to execute the document, at the right-hand side of the page alongside each attestation clause.

The typed deed should be checked extremely carefully, letter-by-letter, and any erasions and alterations made as neatly as possible. Any obvious correction will have to be initialled in the margin by all parties.

Executing the Purchase Deed

The practice is for the purchaser(s) to execute the purchase deed before the vendor(s).

The deed will need to be executed in the presence of a witness. If there are two or more persons incorporated in the same attestation clause, all those mentioned in that clause must execute the deed in the presence of the same witness. With the witness observing, the person executing the deed should sign his name (normal signature is all that is required) alongside the seal. He should then place his finger on the seal and say, 'I deliver this as my act and deed'. The witness should then write details of his name, address and occupation in the space below the attestation clause. An example of how an executed deed might appear is given below.

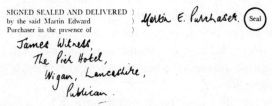

SIGNED SEALED AND DELIVERED)
by the said Martin Edward
Purchaser in the presence of)

Martin E. Purchaser. (Seal)

James Witness,
The Pick Hotel,
Wigan, Lancashire,
Publican.

The executed deed should be sent to the vendor's solicitor for execution by his client.

Where your vendor is to assign to you the benefit of his National House-Building Council House Purchaser's Agreement, at the same time lodge the form of assignment for signature. Leaving the date blank, complete the heading of the form HB12 with details of the vendor (as assignor) and yourself and any other joint purchasers (as transferee). Before the form is sent to the vendor's solicitor, sign it in the presence of a witness. (When the rights under the House Purchaser's Agreement have been transferred to you, you will need to write to the original vendor/ builder, notifying him of the assignment.)

Pre-completion Search and its Results

No earlier than two weeks, and no later than one week, before the date when completion is to take place, apply the instructions given under either (i) or (ii) below depending upon whether the property you are buying has unregistered or registered title.

(i) Property with Unregistered title—Before you complete, you must satisfy yourself that a search of the Central Land Charges Registry has been made against the names of all persons who have owned the property. The abstract of title will have contained details of searches that have been made in the past against previous owners. In the section, 'Investigating the vendor's title', we considered how to determine whether or not you can now rely on those previous searches (see page 62). Where a previous search against a particular name can be relied upon, there is no need for you to repeat it now. The land charges search against the name of the vendor(s) that you made prior to agreeing to buy *must be* repeated now. However, if the pre-contract search also included the names of owners prior to the vendor, it can be relied upon so far as those names are concerned.

Using form K15, you should now make a land charges search against all the relevant names in the manner described in pages 34–36.

If your certificate of result is on form K17, it requires no action on your part and, when the time arrives, you can happily go ahead and complete.

Where the certificate of result is given on form K18, you must consider each entry revealed in line with the comments made in pages 36–40. You may have discovered the entry with your pre-contract search and made the decision then as to what action to take. There is clearly no need to require some evidence that an entry does not relate if that evidence has already been supplied to you in relation to the pre-contract search. Also, if a charge is to be removed as part of the sale to you, your requisitions on title will quite likely have already asked for confirmation that this will be done.

Remember, when you complete, you will be taking the property subject to all charges properly protected by registration. Thus, if you are in any doubt as to the effect of an entry revealed, seek expert assistance.

Whether or not your result of search is on form K17 or K18, you will notice that, at the top right-hand corner of the form, you are told when the protection afforded by that search ends. *Completion must take place before that date.* If for some reason it is apparent that it will not, you cannot rely on this particular result of search; the search *must be repeated.*

(ii) Property with registered title—To make the pre-completion search, one must complete the green, A4 sized, Land Registry form 94A 'Application by Purchaser for Official Search in respect of the whole of land in a title', and its attached duplicate.

All the spaces that must be completed are on the front page of the original and attached duplicate.

The first box should be completed with the name and address of the district Land Registry that dealt with your index map search. Below that, specify the county and district, and the title number. Complete the box 'Full name(s) of the registered pro-prietor(s)'. In the adjoining box, insert the *full* name of yourself and any other person purchasing jointly with you.

Below these boxes, amend the first line of the search request to show that you are making a personal application, by deleting the words in italics. Put an X in the first box of the next line to show that you are a prospective purchaser.

In the middle section of the search request, put an X in the box in the second line thus stating that you are enclosing an authority to inspect the Register. You will have been given this document immediately after exchange of contracts. Locate it now and put it with the form 94A.

The purpose of this search is to discover details of any entries made on the Register since the date on which the copy of it which you have inspected was made. Thus you are required to specify what that date was. You may have examined an official copy made by the Land Registry itself (it will have the words 'office copy' across the top and, at the bottom, the date the copy was made). In such cases, insert the specified date in the appropriate space on form 94A and put an X in the first box. On the other hand, the copy entries in your possession may have been made by the vendor's solicitor from the land certificate in his possession. Here, your 94A search should commence with the date on which the land certificate was prepared, or last brought up to date. This information will have been given in response to requisition on title 3(B)(i). Insert that date in the space on form 94A and put an X in the second of the two boxes.

The search request form should be signed and dated, and your name and address for reply should be inserted, in *block letters*, in the final box.

An example of a completed form 94A is given in Fig 8 on page 87.

The completed form and its duplicate should be sent, with the authority to inspect, to the relevant district Land Registry. No fee is payable.

The result of the search will be endorsed on the reverse side of your application form, and will indicate either that there have been no adverse entries made since the date referred to in your application, or that there have been entries made, details of which are attached.

Where there have been no adverse entries, it means that the official Register is still the same as your copy of it, and you will be safe to complete.

Where entries are revealed by your search, the official Register at the Land Registry is as shown on your copy of it plus the entries revealed by the search. Such additional entries should be considered in exactly the same way as you considered the copy of the Register (see 'Investigating the vendor's title'). Where an entry revealed by your search requires action on the part of the vendor's solicitor, you must acquaint him with the result of your search and obtain his confirmation that he will do all that is necessary. If such confirmation is not forthcoming, or you are in any doubt about the effect of your search result, take legal advice.

Land Registration (Official Searches) Rules, 1969

Application by Purchaser for Official Search in respect of the Whole of the land in a title

(For Official Searches of part of the land in a title, use form 94B)

The attached duplicate must also be completed; a carbon copy will suffice.   **Please see notes overleaf.**

The Chief Land Registrar,
BLANKTOWN District Land Registry,

BLANKTOWN,

BLANKSHIRE.

This panel is printed so that, if desired, the form can be enclosed in a standard window envelope. Please send this application to the appropriate district land registry serving the area in which the property is situated.

(1) *A separate form must be used for each title.*

County and district (or London borough)	Title number(¹)
BLANKSHIRE, NEWTOWN.	BA 123456

Full name(s) of the registered proprietor(s)	Full name(s) of applicant(s) (i.e., purchaser(s), lessee(s) or chargee(s))
ALBERT VENDOR	MARTIN EDWARD PURCHASER

(2) *Where no solicitors are acting, delete as appropriate.*

(3) *Please put an × in the appropriate boxes.*

I/We(²) ~~as solicitor(s) acting for~~ the above-mentioned applicant(s) certify that the applicant(s) intend(s) to

[X] (³)purchase [ ] (³)take on lease [ ] (³)lend money on the security of a registered charge on

the whole of the land comprised in the title above-mentioned.

[ ] (³)I/We also act as solicitors for the registered proprietor(s).

[X] (³)The written authority of the registered proprietor(s) (or his solicitors) to inspect the register accompanies this application.

Application is made for an official search of the register of the above-mentioned title to acertain whether any adverse

entry has been made since 3.7.78 being

[X] (³)the date of the issue of an office copy of the subsisting entries on the register

[ ] (³)the last date on which the land or charge certificate was officially examined with the register.

Signed *M. E. Purchaser.*   Date 5th September 1978

MARTIN EDWARD PURCHASER,	Reference —	This panel must be completed USING BLOCK LETTERS, and inserting the name and address to which the official certificate of result of search is to be sent.
PIER HOTEL,		
WIGAN,	Telephone No. —	
LANCASHIRE.		

Fig 8

You will have noticed that the result of the search specifies a date on which the priority given by it will expire. Your purchase must be completed *and your application for registration of the transfer lodged with the appropriate district land registry* by that date. If it becomes apparent that this will not be possible, you will have to *repeat the search* before you complete.

Executing the Mortgage Deed

When you receive the engrossed mortgage deed, check it against the draft to see that the two agree. If there are any errors, the deed should be returned to the building society's solicitor for correction.

When you have in your possession a correct mortgage deed, it may be executed by you, and any other person with whom you are jointly buying the property, in the manner described in page 83. When this has been done, the executed mortgage deed should be placed in your file to await completion.

Preparing for Completion

You will probably be in a position to make the detailed preparations for completion a week or so before the due date. In any event, your preparations should certainly not be left any later than two or three days before that time.

You will prepare by making the necessary arrangements in relation to when and where completion is to take place. Also, you will need to consider the financial aspects of completion, and give some thought to what you are actually going to be doing.

If you are acting for yourself, not only on a purchase, but also on a simultaneous sale, you are referred to Chapter 15 of this book.

(a) Where and when? The reply to requisition on title 5(A) will have told you where completion is to take place. If you are buying with the aid of a mortgage, not only will you need to attend there, but so also will your building society's solicitor. Therefore, be sure that he knows where he is required to attend, and when.

As to the time of completion, bear in mind that you will

probably not be given a key to the house until you have completed. So, if you are wishing to move into the property on the completion date, you will probably prefer to attend to completion early in the day. With a little 'to-ing and fro-ing', it should be possible to fix a definite appointment to suit all concerned.

If for some reason the vendor is not going to be ready to complete on the agreed date, unfortunately you have no real redress against him for a delay of only a few days or so. Where it is likely that the delay will be longer than just a few days, you should take legal advice.

When you are making arrangements with the vendor's solicitor as to the time and place of completion, clarify the precise arrangements that are being made for delivery of the keys of the property to you. When you pay your purchase money, you are entitled to immediate possession of the property. You may be prepared to allow the vendor a few hours to actually vacate, but you must be sure that, when you complete, the keys are either handed over, or made available to you.

(b) The amount to pay, and how? You should by now have received a completion statement from the vendor's solicitor giving details of the amount required from you. The starting figure in this statement will be the agreed purchase price. Against that you will have been given an allowance for any deposit paid. It may also be that there is some reference made in the statement to general rates, and, in the case of leasehold property, ground rent.

General rates (and water rate, sewerage charges, etc) will be your responsibility as from completion. It is usually the best arrangement for each party to contact the local authority and personally settle their portion of the year's charges. However, where the vendor has already paid more than his share of the year's bill, the most convenient way to correct matters is for you to pay him the amount overpaid. If the rates bill has been apportioned between you and the vendor and an appropriate allowance/charge made in the completion statement, check that the calculation is correct.

Where the property is leasehold, it is normal practice to apportion the ground rent on a daily basis to the completion date. To check such an apportionment, ascertain whether the rent is payable yearly or half-yearly, in advance or in arrear, by looking at your copy of the lease which reserved the rent. Most ground rents are payable in arrear and any apportionment will usually result in an allowance in favour of the purchaser.

On completion, you will want to see the last receipt for the ground rent to satisfy yourself that it has been paid up to date, and to make a note of whom it is payable to.

As you look at the lease to ascertain the position regarding ground rent, also look to see if there is any clause which will require you, after completion, to give notice to the rent owner of the dealing with the property. If so, make a note of its contents and any fee that is payable. Where the lease requires the vendor to obtain prior consent to the assignment, or give notice of the intended sale, you must make a note to obtain the relevant document on completion.

Any inaccuracies in the completion statement should be communicated to the vendor's solicitor immediately and the appropriate correction agreed.

How are you going to pay the amount due from you on completion? If you are financing the purchase from your own funds without the aid of a mortgage, you should make arrangements to have a banker's draft(s) for the amount due, to meet the vendor's requirements (see his reply to your requisition on title 5(C)). Give your bank full details of your requirements (amount, payee's name, etc). In basic terms, a banker's draft is a cheque drawn by the bank on itself. To obtain one you must pay the bank a sum of money to cover the amount of the draft.

If you are providing the purchase price partly from your own funds and partly from a building society loan, you must be sure that the advance from the building society will be received by you in such a form that you can immediately hand it to the vendor's solicitor as payment of the price. Thus, the building society advance should be available in the form of a banker's draft(s) in favour of the vendor's solicitor, or the vendor's building society. The balance of the purchase price which is to come out of your pocket must then be available in such banker's draft(s) as is necessary to meet the vendor's needs. When you have calculated what your requirements are, order the banker's draft(s) from your bank for the money to be provided by you, and make the necessary arrangements with your building society's solicitor.

(c) What to do On completion, you will be doing two main things; satisfying yourself that the vendor is in reality the owner of the property, and making sure that ownership will be transferred to you. As you work through the following pages where the steps to be taken on completion are considered, prepare a check-list of what you must do.

When you investigated title, you were only examining *copies* of the documents that prove the ownership of the property. On completion, you will want to see the *original* documents. (It should be remembered that, in some cases, the vendor may not have the original of a particular document, but only a marked abstract of it, eg, where the property consists of only part of the property dealt with by that deed).

Thus, in the case of property with unregistered title, prepare for completion by gathering together all the documents, plans etc, that comprise the abstract of title. When you have done this, consider, in relation to each abstracted deed or event, what proof of that occurrence you will be given on completion (eg, production of the original deed, or a marked abstract of it). The reply to requisition on title 3(A) will no doubt prove helpful in this regard. Proof of such events as, eg, marriage, is given by the production of a copy of the appropriate certificate issued by the Registrar of Births, Deaths, and Marriages.

So far as property with registered title is concerned, you should locate the copy of the Register that the vendor supplied to you. On completion, you will be comparing this with the official land certificate (or charge certificate, where there is a mortgage of the property). If the Register is not complete in itself but refers to and incorporates some other document, eg, a deed in which restrictive covenants are set out, or, in the case of leasehold property, the lease, a copy of which has been supplied to you, such copy of that document should be put with the copy entries. You need to determine in advance what you are going to compare that copy against to verify its accuracy (ie, whether the original, or a marked copy).

Whether you are dealing with registered or unregistered title, make a note to obtain any other additional evidence that you stipulated must be given to you to resolve any apparent problem relating to the vendor's ownership, eg, arising from the investigation of title, or your searches. Where the property is held by the vendor subject to a mortgage, one such document will be the vacating receipt (or form of discharge, where the title is registered) in respect of that mortgage.

To ensure that on completion you will become the owner of the property, make a note to remind yourself to collect the purchase deed duly executed by the vendor.

Other ancillary matters that should be dealt with on completion could include collecting the NHBC Certificate, and House Purchaser's Agreement (with the vendor's assignment of the same to you), and inspecting the last receipt for general rates, ground rent, etc.

An example of a typical completion check-list is given below.

1 Compare abstract of title (or copy entries, if the title is registered) with originals.

2 Collect originals of abstracted deeds (or land/charge certificate, if the title is registered).

3 Collect signed vacating receipt (or form of discharge, where the title is registered) in respect of the mortgage dated . . .

4 Obtain vendor's solicitor's certification that entry revealed by land charges search does not relate.

5 Obtain signed application for cancellation of registration protecting the rights of the vendor's spouse to occupy the matrimonial home.

6 Collect NHBC Certificate, Agreement, and assignment.

7 Examine last receipts for ground rent, and general rates.

8 Collect purchase deed executed by vendor.

9 Collect keys.

10 Hand over banker's draft(s).

If you are buying property with the assistance of a mortgage, you must also make a note to remind yourself to do all that will be necessary to secure the release of the building society loan.

On completion, the building society's solicitor will want to check the documents being given to you by the vendor to make sure that you will in fact be becoming the legal owner of the property, and thus able to grant a mortgage to his client. When satisfied that this is the case, he will give you the appropriate banker's draft(s) for the amount of the loan in exchange for all the title deeds of the property (which the building society will keep as security), and the mortgage deed executed by you.

In later pages of this book we discuss what action a purchaser should take once the matter has been completed. This includes delivering the purchase deed to the Inland Revenue and (perhaps) lodging the documents with the Land Registry. You will not be able to attend to these matters yourself if you have parted with the deeds. Thus, you will need to give the building society's solicitor, on completion, all the necessary completed forms and requisite fees to enable him to attend to these post-completion matters. So, if you are buying the property with the aid of a mortgage, you must *now* prepare such forms described in pages 97–111 of this book as are appropriate. If stamp duty is payable on the purchase deed, a cheque for the duty will have to be given to the building society's solicitor. You must also be ready to hand him a cheque in favour of 'HM Land Registry' to cover any Land Registry fees that will be payable.

Thus, where you will be mortgaging the property, your checklist may need to be extended as follows:

11 Hand to the building society's solicitor all title deeds and documents relating to the property together with the purchase deed and mortgage deed.

12 Collect banker's draft(s) for the building society loan (hand to the vendor's solicitor).

13 Hand to the building society's solicitor completed form L(A) 451.

(Also, in cases where the disposition will need to be registered:)

14 Hand to the building society's solicitor completed Land Registry form(s) and cheque for the fees.

There is only one more matter to be attended to before you are ready to complete. You must inspect the property to see that, if it is supposed to be vacant, that is in fact the case, and that, in any event, there are no strange people in occupation or otherwise claiming rights over the property. If the property does not appear to be as it should, you cannot consider completing your purchase until the problem has been resolved. Discuss the matter with the vendor's solicitor (and, if necessary, with the vendor). If you are still in doubt as to whether or not you will obtain vacant possession on completion, obtain legal advice.

7 Completion

In broad terms, all you will be doing on completion is working through your check-list and making sure that every task is dealt with.

First of all you will be comparing the abstract of title with the original deeds or, in the case of property with registered title, comparing the copy entries with the land/charge certificate. To do this, you must be able to recognise the original.

An original deed will usually be on thick, parchment-type paper, and is actually signed, sealed, and delivered by the parties to it. So, as you look at the document before you, make sure that it bears the original signatures of the persons concerned. (Where the document is one which would need to have been delivered to the Inland Revenue, the actual ink stamp marks at the top of the first page will identify the original.)

On completion, you must check all particulars of the deed, eg, stamping, contents, due execution, etc, and make sure that all vacating receipts on mortgages have been properly signed.

The original of a land/charge certificate is about 10 x 15in in size, and is prepared in the form of a book with the pages of the certificate stitched inside a stout cover which bears the title 'Land Certificate' or 'Charge Certificate'. On the inside of the front cover there is a Land Registry stamp indicating the date when the certificate was last made to agree with the Register, and alongside each entry is the original oval Land Registry authenticating stamp.

If the vendor owns registered title subject to a mortgage, on completion you will be collecting a form of discharge of the charge (form 53). This is simply a document by which the owner of the charge admits that it has been discharged. Check that the details of the property and title as given on the form are correct, and that it has been dated and signed by the proprietor of the charge in the presence of a witness. A building society must have impressed its seal in the presence of (and witnessed by) a person authorised for that purpose by the board of directors, or committee of management.

On completion, when you indicate that you are satisfied that the vendor really owns the property, the vendor's solicitor will date the purchase deed and give this to you in exchange for the balance of the purchase money. Make sure that it is the document that you prepared (you should be able to recognise your handiwork at a glance!) and that it has been signed, sealed and delivered by the vendor. You will also be given the original title documents to the property, and the keys.

If you are not buying with the aid of a mortgage, that will be the end of completion. The house is now yours!

Where you are buying with the aid of a mortgage, you must then date the executed mortgage deed with the same date as the purchase deed. Before you hand the original mortgage (with the purchase deed and the title deeds to the property) to the building society's solicitor, complete your draft copies of the mortgage and the purchase deed.

The building society's solicitor must also be given the completed form L(A) 451 (with the date of the purchase deed inserted in box 2) duly signed and dated, together with a cheque for any duty payable.

Where title to the property is already registered, the completed and signed Land Registry form A4, together with a cheque for the fees, should be given to the building society's solicitor with a certified copy of the deed of transfer.

Where title to the property is not actually registered but it is in an area of compulsory registration, date and sign the Land Registry A13 forms and hand them to the building society's solicitor with a cheque for the fees payable. When you have completed the blank spaces on pages 1 and 2 of the application form 1A (or 2A), the building society's solicitor will require you (and any other co-purchaser) to accompany him to the offices of a commissioner for oaths to 'swear' the declaration on pages 2 and 3. The form will then be left with the building society's solicitor.

8 After Completion

General Considerations

Even though you have completed your purchase, your work as a conveyancer is not yet over. The purchase deed must be delivered to the Inland Revenue, you may have to arrange for land charges to be cancelled, and the transaction may need to be registered at HM Land Registry. None of these tasks can be left indefinitely since strict time limits are involved. Thus, no later than a couple of days after completion, you must start to attend to the matters described below.

Stamping of the Purchase Deed

The deed transferring ownership of the property to you must be produced to the Inland Revenue authorities accompanied by a completed Inland Revenue form L(A) 451. At the same time, you will be required to pay any stamp duty chargeable on the deed. If the price you paid for the property was not more than £15,000 and the deed contains a certificate of value in that amount, no duty is payable. In any other case, duty is payable in accordance with the rates set out in Table 11 on page 164.

An example of a completed form L(A) 451 is given in Fig 9 on page 99.

The form has two duplicates attached. Each sheet has been specially treated and no carbon paper is required to make the copies.

If the deed is an assignment, or a transfer (as opposed to a conveyance), describe it as such in box 1.

If you have bought leasehold property, box 6 should be completed along the following lines, 'Assignment of residue of a lease for a term of 999 years from 1/1/30 at a yearly rent of £5'.

In box 7(a), put the price you paid for the property. In reply to 7(b)–(f), 8, and 9, you will usually be able to put the stock answers as given in the specimen.

The completed form and its white duplicate (the yellow copy being for your use), together with the purchase deed and your remittance for any duty payable should be taken to one of the Inland Revenue stamp offices (addresses, page 153), or, alternatively, handed in at any Head Post Office.

While you are waiting for the deed to be stamped, apply the next section, where relevant.

Cancellation of Land Charges

The comments contained here are applicable only where your vendor held property with unregistered title subject to a registered land charge which he undertook to remove as part of the sale to you (eg, registrations of class C(i), C(iii), and F). On completion you will have been given a completed and signed form of application for cancellation of the registration. (If you bought with the aid of a mortgage, you will have delivered this form to the building society's solicitor and he will now be attending to the procedure here described.)

The completed form of application for cancellation must be sent to the land charges department at Plymouth. In due course, you will receive an official computer print-out acknowledgement (form K22) confirming that the entry has been removed from the Index of Charges. This acknowledgement should be attached to the K18 search result that revealed the entry concerned.

PARTICULARS OF INSTRUMENTS TRANSFERRING OR LEASING LAND

FINANCE ACT 1931
as amended by the Land Commission Act, 1967

ATTENTION IS DRAWN TO THE NOTES OVERLEAF

FOR OFFICIAL USE

V.O. No. _____

Map Ref. _____

File _____

Code/Dscptn _____

GV/RV _____

Return _____

HPPR: Qtr./ }
Yr. etc. }

Other _____

This is a three-part form: the third part on yellow paper is for your retention, but the two parts on white paper should NOT be separated. Please use a TYPEWRITER or BALL-POINT PEN applied firmly. **NO CARBON PAPER IS REQUIRED.**

I. Description of Instrument: CONVEYANCE	**2. Date of Instrument:** 10th SEPTEMBER 1978
3. Name and Address of Transferor or Lessor: (BLOCK LETTERS) ALBERT VENDOR, 1, MAIN STREET, NEWTOWN, BLANKSHIRE.	**4. Name and Address of Transferee or Lessee: (BLOCK LETTERS)** MARTIN EDWARD PURCHASER, PIER HOTEL, WIGAN, LANCASHIRE.

5. SITUATION OF THE LAND. Sufficient information must be given to enable the land to be identified accurately, e.g., by including any dimensions stated in the instrument and by attaching a plan to this form or by describing the boundaries in full. For premises the full postal address is sufficient.

1, MAIN STREET, NEWTOWN.

COUNTY _____ BLANKSHIRE _____ RATING AUTHORITY _____ NEWTOWN DISTRICT COUNCIL

6. ESTATE OR INTEREST TRANSFERRED. Where the transaction is the assignment or grant of a lease, or the transfer of a fee simple subject to a lease, the terms of the lease, the date of commencement of the term and the rent reserved must be stated.

FEE SIMPLE

7. CONSIDERATION State separately: (a) any capital payment, with the date when due if otherwise than on execution of the instrument: £11,500	**8.** Any MINERALS, MINERAL RIGHTS, SPORTING RIGHTS, TIMBER or EASEMENTS reserved: (on a separate sheet if necessary). NONE OTHER THAN THE USUAL
(b) any debt released, covenanted to be paid or to which the transaction is made subject: NONE	
(c) any periodical payment (including any charge) covenanted to be paid: NONE	**9.** Any RESTRICTIONS, COVENANTS OR CONDITIONS affecting the value of the estate or interest transferred or granted: (on a separate sheet if necessary). NONE ONEROUS
(d) any terms surrendered: NONE	
(e) any land exchanged: NONE	**10. SIGNATURE of Transferee or Lessee or person on his behalf:**
(f) any other thing representing money or money's worth: NONE	*M. E. Purchaser.* Date 13.9.78.
II. Name and Address of Transferor's or Lessor's Solicitor: (BLOCK LETTERS) SMITH & CO. 24, PARK LANE, NEWTOWN, BLANKSHIRE.	**12. Name and Address of Signatory if other than Transferee or Lessee: (BLOCK LETTERS)** N/A

STAMPS L(A) 451

Fig 9

Registration of the Disposition

There are two cases where the sale to you will have to be registered at HM Land Registry: where title to the property is not yet registered but the property is in an area of compulsory registration of title, and where title is already registered.

(a) Compulsory registration of unregistered title—In applying for first registration of title, you will be required to lodge at the Land Registry all your documents of title. These will be examined and, if the Land Registry is satisfied that you have legal title to the land, you will be registered as proprietor and a land certificate (or charge certificate, where the property is subject to a registered mortgage) will be issued.

Gather together all the documents that prove your ownership of the property, ie, all deeds, abstracts, search certificates, etc, that you received from the vendor, together with the deed transferring the property to you. Put with these documents your local search, contract, requisitions on title and replies, index map search, and your land charges searches (together with any certificate of cancellation of any entry revealed). It is also necessary to lodge a certified true copy of the purchase deed. The carbon copy that you took when engrossing the deed (completed with the date and details of execution) may be used for this purpose. At the top write, 'I certify this to be a true copy of the original'. This certification should be signed by you and any other co-purchaser.

These documents should be listed, in chronological order, on Land Registry form A13 in triplicate (with a carbon copy on plain paper for your file). At the top of the form, enter your name and address, and the address of the property. The space for the title number should be left blank.

Where you are buying property with the assistance of a mortgage and are completing the registration forms in advance of completion, the list that you are now preparing must include those deeds, abstracts, etc, that you will be receiving later (see the answer to requisition on title 3A). If you are in any doubt as to precisely what the vendor's solicitor will hand over on completion, telephone him and request the necessary information. The list of documents must include the purchase deed transferring ownership to you and the certified copy which must accompany your application. The last two entries on the list of documents will be the mortgage deed, and certified copy mortgage (which the building society's solicitor will provide).

All three copies of the form should be signed by yourself and any other co-purchaser.

You must now complete your form of application for first registration, form 1A (or 2A, if the property is leasehold).

The last page of the form is for official use only and can be ignored. An example of a completed form 1A is set out in Fig 10 on pages 102–104. Form 2A is completed along similar lines.

Details of the property are to be given first. You must then enter details of the fee payable, calculated according to the following scale.

Value of land	*Fee*
Not exceeding £10,000	£1.70 for every £1,000 or part of £1,000
Exceeding £10,000 but not exceeding £100,000	£17 for the first £10,000 and £1.50 for every £1,000 or part of £1,000 over £10,000
Exceeding £100,000	£152 for the first £100,000 and £0.25 for every £1,000 or part of £1,000 over £100,000 with a maximum fee of £314.50

Enter the price you paid for the property in the 'Value' column, and, using that figure, calculate the fee and enter it in the 'Fees' column. Ignore 'Other fees'. (No fees are payable on any mortgage which is being lodged for registration with your application.)

You must now work through the remainder of the first page and the first half of the second page of the form giving full details of the name(s) and address(es) of yourself and any other co-purchaser(s), and completing all blanks as appropriate.

Form 1A

H.M. Land Registry

Land Registration Acts, 1925 to 1971

APPLICATION BY OWNER(S) FOR FIRST REGISTRATION OF FREEHOLD LAND —NO SOLICITOR ACTING

FOR OFFICIAL USE ONLY		
Date stamp	Title number	Fee stamp

Details in the panels below to be supplied by applicant

PROPERTY

County and District (or London borough)} BLANKSHIRE, NEWTOWN.

Short description 1, MAIN STREET, NEWTOWN, BLANKSHIRE.
(including parish or place)

LAND REGISTRY FEES

Notes:
1. Fees are assessed under the Land Registration Fee Order 1970 as amended by the Land Registration Fee Order 1973, and are payable on the delivery of applications.
2. Cheques should be made payable to the "Land Registry".
3. No fee is payable for the registration of any charge or mortgage by the applicant that accompanies this application.

	Value £	Fee Scale	Land Registry Fees £	Particulars of underpayments or overpayments
Land and buildings	£11,500		20 -	
Other fees (As to charges and mortgages see note 3 above)		Total fees paid	- -	
			£20 -	

I/WE MARTIN EDWARD PURCHASER, OF 1, MAIN STREET, NEWTOWN,
(In BLOCK LETTERS, full name(s), address(es) and occupation(s) for entry on the register)

BLANKSHIRE, TEACHER

hereby apply for registration as proprietor(s), with **Absolute** title, of the freehold land described above assured by the accompanying [1]*conveyance/transfer* dated 10th SEPTEMBER 1978 made between:

(1) *Strike out or amend as appropriate.*

(1) ALBERT VENDOR

(2) MARTIN EDWARD PURCHASER

( )

( )

1. I/We purchased the land from the said ALBERT VENDOR

on 10th SEPTEMBER 1978 and paid the whole of the purchase money

(2) *Or otherwise as the case may be.*

of £ 11,500 to him/them [2] *Messrs*

of

solicitors, acted as my/our solicitors in the purchase but are not carrying out this registration on my/our behalf.

(OVER)

Fig 10

2. The deeds and documents accompanying this application and mentioned in the accompanying

list in triplicate signed by me/~~us~~ and dated the _____20th~~ of SEPTEMBER _____ 19 78
are all the deeds and documents relating to the title which I/~~we~~ have in my/~~our~~ possession or under
my/~~our~~ control, including opinions of counsel, abstracts, contracts for sale, requisitions, replies,
official certificates of search in the Land Charges Department and other like documents in regard
to the title.

3. (a) Any abstracts of title lodged herewith are marked as verified by the solicitors who
examined them with the original deeds and all particulars of wills, grants of probate or letters of
administration, marriages and deaths set out therein as separate items are also marked as verified
by the solicitor concerned. Such abstracts contain a copy or full extract of all restrictive covenants,
stipulations and easements to which the land is subject, similarly marked as examined.

(b) (1)None of the/~~Only the following~~ entries disclosed in the certificates of official search in
the Land Charges Department lodged herewith or referred to in an abstract of title affect the land:

~~(1) The instruments creating the entries are those dated~~

~~which, or abstracts of which, accompany this application~~

~~4. (2) I/We hereby apply that no note be made on the register of the lease dated~~

~~which has been determined by merger. I/We declare that I am/we are not~~
~~aware of any (3) sub lease or other incumbrance affecting the said lease.~~

Signature~~s~~ of the applicant~~s~~   M. E. Pulchaser.

Date   20th SEPTEMBER 1978

STATUTORY DECLARATION IN SUPPORT
To be sworn before a Commissioner for Oaths or Justice of the Peace

(1)I/~~We~~ the above named applicant~~s~~, (1)~~do severally,~~ solemnly and sincerely declare that

(a) (4)I (being a sole owner) am entitled to the land for my own benefit.

—OR—

~~(a) (4) We (being joint owners) are entitled to the land holding for ourselves as:~~
~~(5) ☐ beneficial joint tenants   (5) ☐ tenants in common~~

—OR—

~~(a) (4) I am/We are entitled to the land as estate owner(s) within the meaning of section 1~~
~~of the Land Registration Act, 1925, as (6)~~

(b) (1)I/~~We~~ have been since the date of the (1)conveyance/~~transfer~~ dated 10th SEPTEMBER
1978 _____ and (1)I/~~we~~ still (1)am/~~are~~ in undisputed possession of the land comprised in
the application and there is no person in occupation thereof or any part thereof adversely to (1)my/~~our~~
estate or interest therein.

(c) (1)I/~~We~~ have not entered into or created and the land is not subject to any contract for sale,
lease or agreement for lease, easement, mortgage, charge, lien, rentcharge, restrictive covenant or other
right or incumbrance except as stated in the (1)conveyance/~~transfer~~ dated 10th SEPTEMBER
1978 _____ or in the schedule below affecting the land or any part thereof.

(d) All deeds, wills and instruments of title, and all charges and incumbrances, as well as all
facts material to the title, have been disclosed in the application and (1)I am/~~we are~~ not aware of any
question or doubt affecting the title to the land or any part thereof or of any matter or thing whereby
the title is or may be impeached, affected or called in question in any manner whatsoever.

(e) The present value of the land with all buildings thereon does not exceed £ 11,500.

THE SCHEDULE OF INCUMBRANCES

**(This schedule should include any incumbrances of the kinds mentioned in paragraph (c) of this
declaration above which affect the land including any charges created by the applicant(s). If there are
no such incumbrances, enter the word "NONE" below.**

MORTGAGE dated 10th September 1978 - the Applicant (1)

   Biggest Building Society (2).

(1) *I/We* make this solemn declaration conscientiously believing the same to be true and by virtue of the Statutory Declarations Act, 1835.

Declared by the said..

.... *and*

....

at..

in the county of..

this..........day of.............................. 19...,

before me,

Name..

Address..

Qualification..

INSTRUCTIONS REGARDING DOCUMENTS

To ensure that acknowledgments are sent to the correct person and that documents are issued to the persons entitled to have them, **IT IS IMPORTANT THAT PANELS 1, 2 AND 3 BELOW ARE COMPLETED CORRECTLY.**

1. Documents enclosed...   ...   .
   (*Strike out or add as required*)

1. *Conveyance/~~Transfer~~ to applicant*.

2. Certified copy of same.

3. *Charge by applicant*.

4. *Certified copy of same.*

5. Documents (including the foregoing) set out on *list in triplicate* herewith.

2. Name and address of person to whom the acknowledgment of the application and all requisitions made by the Land Registry, including requests for unpaid fees, are to be sent:

BLOCK LETTERS

Name   MARTIN EDWARD PURCHASER,

Address   1, MAIN STREET,

NEWTOWN, BLANKSHIRE.

Reference   -   Telephone number Newtown 1234

IMPORTANT

The documents not retained in the Land Registry, together with the land certificate (or charge certificate(s) as the case may be) will, on the completion of the registration, be returned to the above address. If a particular document is required to be issued to some other person or firm, upon completion of the registration or in connection with any requisition which may arise, please complete panel 3 below.

3. Additional instructions (if any) for the issue of any document to some person or firm other than that mentioned in panel 2 above:

BLOCK LETTERS

Description of document ALL DOCUMENTS

Name   JONES & CO.

Address   13, HIGH STREET,

NEWTOWN, BLANKSHIRE.

Reference   S/1   Telephone number Newtown 5678

Fig 10

(If you are completing this form in advance of completion for handing to the building society's solicitor, you will have to leave blank the references in the form to the dates of the purchase deed, and the list of documents.)

On page 2, in item 3(b), delete one or other of the opening phrases depending upon whether there are, or are not, entries revealed by your land charges search that affect the property. If there are none, delete the concluding words. Where there are land charges that affect the property (eg, a D(ii) entry in respect of a restrictive covenant), delete the opening words 'None of the', enter details of the land charge in the space provided, and insert the date of the document creating the land charge in the next phrase.

Item 4 will usually be inapplicable and may be deleted.

The form should be signed by yourself and any other co-purchaser and dated. (*Do not* date the form where you are preparing it in advance of completion for handing to your building society's solicitor.)

You must now prepare the statutory declaration in support of your application. This is set out on the second half of page 2, and the first half of page 3 of the form.

In (a) only one of the three options will be appropriate. This will either be the first, if you are a sole purchaser, or the second, if you are a joint purchaser with some other person(s) and you hold the property as joint tenants.

Enter the date of the purchase deed in (b), and also in (c). In (o), the words '*or in the schedule below*' should be deleted if you bought the property without the aid of a mortgage. If you are buying with the aid of a mortgage, do not delete these words but rather enter details of the mortgage (title, date, and parties) in the schedule at the bottom of the page. (Where there is a mortgage and you are preparing the Land Registry forms in advance of completion, you will not be able to enter the dates of the purchase deed and mortgage in items (b) and (c) of the statutory declaration and the schedule).

In (e), enter the price you paid for the property.

The portion on page 3 dealing with the signing and making of the statutory declaration should *not be completed.*

Finally, give the Land Registry your instructions regarding the documents of title by completing the boxes on the second half of page 3. In box 1, delete any reference to a document that is not being lodged, eg, a charge if you purchased without a mortgage. Where you are completing form 2A, the reference to the lease may need to be deleted if all you have is a marked abstract of it. In box 2, enter your name and address, and telephone number. Where you are buying the property with the aid of a mortgage, enter the name and address, and telephone number of the building society's solicitor in box 3, and next to the words, 'Description of document' enter 'all documents'. If you have not granted a mortgage of your property, box 3 can be ruled through.

Once the form has been completed, it must be 'sworn' before it can be sent to the Registry. You 'swear' the document by taking it along to a commissioner for oaths, or justice of the peace and swearing before him that the contents of your statutory declaration are true. This declaration must be made by yourself and any other co-purchaser(s). All practising solicitors are able to act as a commissioner for oaths. Attend to this requirement now.

Where you are buying with the aid of a mortgage and are preparing the forms in advance of completion, you *cannot* have the declaration sworn now. On completion you will be required to go along with the building society's solicitor to have the papers sworn. (This will mean that not only must you attend at completion, but so also must any other person who is buying the property jointly with you.)

The form, duly completed and sworn, together with the deeds and any other documents of title, the A13 forms in triplicate, and a cheque in favour of HM Land Registry for the fees payable, should be sent (registered post) to the district Land Registry serving the area in which the property is situated.

When your application is received, it will be acknowledged, and the investigation of your claim to ownership will commence. As part of this process, the Land Registry may notify you that it is arranging for a survey to establish boundaries. Such a communication requires no action on your part. Further, the Land

Registry may submit requisitions on title which you will have to answer if you wish your application for registration to proceed. Where you bought with the aid of a mortgage, the building society's solicitor may be able to help you formulate suitable replies.

(b) Registration of a dealing with a registered title—To have your name entered on the register as the proprietor of the title in substitution for the name of the vendor, it is necessary to lodge at the Land Registry a completed form A4 together with the appropriate fees. Only pages 1 and 4 of this form concern you. An example of a completed form is set out in Fig 11 on pages 108 and 109.

In the first section, enter details of the property and the title number. Below this, insert particulars of the application, ie, 'transfer', and alongside it the price you have paid. A fee is payable to the Land Registry for registering the dealing calculated according to the following scale.

Value of Land	*Fee*
Not exceeding £20,000	£2.50 for every £1,000 or part of £1,000
Exceeding £20,000 but not exceeding £100,000	£50 for the first £20,000 and £2.40 for every £1,000 or part of £1,000 over £20,000
Exceeding £100,000	£242 for the first £100,000 and £0.50 for every £1,000 or part of £1,000 over £100,000 with a maximum fee of £567

Using the price you paid for the house, apply the scale to ascertain the fee. This should then be entered in the appropriate column.

If you are buying the property with the aid of a mortgage, enter 'mortgage' and the amount of the loan on the next line. No fee is payable for registering a mortgage which accompanies a transfer for value. Enter details of the total fee being paid.

In panel 1, give particulars of all the documents that you

H.M. LAND REGISTRY

APPLICATION FOR REGISTRATION OF DEALINGS WITH THE WHOLE OF THE LAND COMPRISED IN ONE OR MORE REGISTERED TITLES

FOR OFFICIAL USE ONLY		
Date stamp	Application number	Fee stamp

THE PANELS BELOW SHOULD BE COMPLETED BY THE APPLICANT OR HIS SOLICITOR.

By post or under hand
Received Stamp
Ackd. by
Date

County and District (or London borough)	Title number(s) (1)	Pending application numbers
BLANKSHIRE, NEWTOWN	BA 123456	
	–	
(1) If this application affects more than eight title numbers, attach a separate list of them (in triplicate) to this page and write "see list" in the space opposite	–	
	–	
	–	
	–	
	–	

Nature and priority of applications	Value	Fee scale, para. or abatement	Fees paid (2) £	Particulars of underpayments or overpayments
TRANSFER	£11,500		30 –	
MORTGAGE	£7,500		– –	
Total Land Registry fees paid			£30 –	

(2) Fees are assessed under the Land Registration Fee Order, 1970, as amended by the Land Registration Fee Order, 1971, and should be paid on delivery of applications. They may be paid by cheque, postal order or money order, drawn in favour of "H.M. Land Registry" or by Land Registry adhesive stamps where the amount is small.

Panel 1

DOCUMENTS LODGED HEREWITH
Please list all documents (originals and copies to be treated as separate items)

(i) CHARGE CERTIF.	(iv) COPY TRANSFER.	(vii) SEARCH 94A.
(ii) FORM 53.	(v) CHARGE.	(viii) –
(iii) TRANSFER.	(vi) COPY CHARGE.	(ix) –

Name and address of solicitor or applicant to whom the acknowledgment of the application and all requisitions made by the Land Registry including requests for unpaid fees are to be sent:

BLOCK LETTERS

Name MARTIN EDWARD PURCHASER,

Address 1, MAIN STREET,

NEWTOWN, BLANKSHIRE.

Solicitor's reference – Telephone number Newtown 1234.

IMPORTANT

The documents not retained in the Land Registry, together with the land certificate (or charge certificate(s) as the case may be), will, on the completion of the registration, be returned to the above address. If a particular document is required to be issued to some other person or firm upon completion of the registration or in connection with any requisition which may arise, please complete panel 2 below.

Panel 2 Additional instructions (if any) for return of any document to some person or firm other than that mentioned in panel 1 above:

BLOCK LETTERS

Description of document ALL DOCUMENTS

Name JONES & CO.

Address 13, HIGH STREET, NEWTOWN, BLANKSHIRE.

Reference 3/1

THE PARTICULARS REQUESTED ON PAGE 4 MUST ALSO BE SUPPLIED

3. **Full Postal address** (including any postal code) for entry on the register is:

As to new proprietor(s) of the land (if any)	As to new proprietor(s) of a charge (if any)
1, MAIN STREET,	BOUNTY HOUSE,
NEWTOWN,	BACK STREET,
BLANKSHIRE.	NEWTOWN, BLANKSHIRE.

4. IF THE TRANSFER OR ASSENT IS TO JOINT TENANTS it should be stated whether or not the survivor of them can give a valid receipt for capital money arising on a disposition of the land.   [YES]   (State YES or NO)

5. ON APPLYING TO REGISTER A COMPANY(1) AS PROPRIETOR OF LAND OR OF A CHARGE, a copy of the memorandum and articles of association, certified as a true copy by the secretary or solicitor of the company, should be produced (rule 259). However, production can usually be dispensed with if the company's solicitor supplies the following confirmation.

(A) (ON APPLYING TO REGISTER A COMPANY AS PROPRIETOR OF LAND)

We, solicitors to _____ Limited, hereby confirm that:
(insert name of company)

(a) the company is a company trading for profit and has been incorporated in England or Scotland under the Companies Acts;

(b) the memorandum and articles of association contains provisions entitling the company to hold and sell, mortgage, lease and otherwise deal with land and to borrow, lend and invest money;

(2)(c) the charge(s) by the company lodged herewith do(es) not contravene any of the provisions of the memorandum and articles of association of the company.

Signature of company's solicitor _____

(B) (ON APPLYING TO REGISTER A COMPANY AS PROPRIETOR OF A CHARGE)

We, solicitors to _____ Limited, hereby confirm that:
(insert name of company)

(a) the company is a company trading for profit and has been incorporated in England or Scotland under the Companies Acts;

(b) the memorandum and articles of association contains provisions entitling the company to hold and sell, mortgage, lease and otherwise deal with land and to borrow, lend and invest money;

(c) the lending of money:

(2)is not the primary object of the company and the company is not a moneylender as defined in the Moneylenders Act, 1900, s. 6.

or

(2)is the primary object of the company and the company holds a moneylender's excise licence and

(i) a note or memorandum in writing of the contract was signed by the borrower and a copy of it was delivered to him pursuant to section 6 of the Moneylenders Act, 1927;

(ii) there has been no contravention of any of the other provisions of the said Act, in connection with the transaction to which the charge relates.

or

(2)is the primary object of the company but the company is exempt from the provisions of the Moneylenders Acts because _____
(Here give the grounds of the exemption, e.g., that the company carries on the business of banking, or has an exemption order of the Department of Trade and Industry.)

Signature of company's solicitors _____

(1) The term "company" is here used to refer to companies registered under the Companies Acts.
(2) Strike out if inapplicable.

6. IF A DISCHARGE OF THE ONLY REMAINING CHARGE. As solicitors for the registered proprietor of the land, we hereby apply for the issue of the land certificate to us.

Signature _____

REMINDERS

Please see that:

1. Charges are accompanied by copies certified by a solicitor (or in the name of the firm) as true copies. **Certification by clerks is not sufficient.**

2. **All material dates and particulars have been inserted in charges especially in the printed forms of building society and insurance company mortgages.**

3. Evidence of death or change of name is lodged where required.

4. The lease is lodged in support of an application for merger.

I/We have supplied the information required and hereby apply for the registration of the dealings in the order of priority shown on page 1 and request that, if practicable, the register be cleared so as to show only subsisting entries. *A cheque, postal order, money order or Land Registry adhesive stamps, value* £30, _____ *accompanies this application.*

Signature of applicant or his solicitors   *M. E. Purchaser.*   Date 20th September 1978

Printed in England by Lowes Limited, Southport and published by Her Majesty's Stationery Office
2½p net or 25 for 45p net (exclusive of tax)
Dd 504372 K2400 7/73 Gp 1664
SBN 11 390077 5

Fig 11

are lodging in support of your application, ie, the land (or charge) certificate, the transfer to you (and a certified copy of it), your form 94A search, and any mortgage by you (together with a certified copy). Other documents which may need to accompany your application could include a form of discharge for any existing mortgage (form 53), evidence of the change of name of the proprietor (eg, on marriage), and applications for the removal of an entry protecting the rights of the vendor's spouse to occupy the matrimonial home. For the copy transfer, use the carbon copy you took when engrossing the purchase deed. Complete this with details of the date and execution, and write across the top, 'I certify this to be a true copy of the original'. This certification should be signed by yourself and any other co-purchaser(s).

If you are completing the form in advance of completion ready for handing to the building society's solicitor, you will not have in your possession the mortgage deed or a copy of it. However, complete the form as though you do. In due course, these documents will be placed with the application form by the building society's solicitor before he sends it to the Registry.

In the second half of panel 1, enter your name, address and telephone number.

Where you are buying the property with the aid of a mortgage, the name and address of the building society's solicitor must be entered in panel 2. Alongside 'Description of document' enter 'all documents'. If you bought without a mortgage loan, panel 2 can be ruled through.

Turning to the back page, insert the full postal address of yourself and the registered office of your building society (if any) in panel 3. Where you bought the property jointly with another, enter 'yes' or 'no' in the box in panel 4 according to whether or not the survivor of you is to have the power to dispose of the property (see the penultimate clause in the deed of transfer). Panels 5 and 6 may be deleted in full.

Finally, enter the amount of any cheque enclosed to cover fees payable, and date the form which should then be signed by yourself and any co-purchaser(s).

If you are buying with the aid of a mortgage and are filling in the form in advance of completion, it should not be dated yet, but it is wise to have any co-purchaser sign it now so that there will be no need for them personally to attend on completion.

The completed form together with all the accompanying documents and a cheque in favour of HM Land Registry to cover the fees should be sent, registered post, to the district Land Registry serving the area in which the property is situated.

Notices of Change of Ownership

In your requisitions on title (number 7, notices), you asked the vendor's solicitor for details of the name and address of any person to whom notice of the transfer of ownership must be given. Normally, the only situation where this is necessary is where the property is leasehold and the lease stipulates that such notice must be given. Often, the lease stipulates that a fee is payable for dealing with the notice.

Where you are required to give notice of the change of ownership, write to the person concerned (usually the collector of the rent reserved by the lease), giving details of the property (and the lease, if any), and stating that you are the new owner. Enclose your remittance for any fee payable. Send a top and a carbon copy of this letter with a request that the duplicate be returned receipted.

When it is received, the receipted duplicate should be placed with the title deeds as evidence that the requirement of the lease has been complied with. If you have handed your deeds to your building society's solicitor, the duplicate notice should now be sent to him.

Custody of Documents

Where you bought the property with the aid of a mortgage, the building society will retain the title documents for so long as there remains money outstanding, so the problem of what you should do with them will only arise at that distant, future time.

If you did not have a mortgage and the disposition was registered at HM Land Registry, you will ultimately have received a land certificate. Check that it is correct and that the date it was prepared/amended in your favour has been stamped on the inside of the front cover. If any inaccuracy is discovered, *do not* attempt to correct it yourself. The land certificate will have to be returned to the Land Registry.

Ideally, you should keep the deeds in a fireproof safe. This will normally mean that you will have to ask your bank to keep them for you. They will usually be quite willing to do this. All the documents of title, including any search certificates, land charges cancellation certificates, notice of assignment, etc, should be placed in a stout envelope, or wrapped, and tied round with tape or string. Label the packet with details of its contents. When you take the title documents to the bank for safe custody obtain a receipt and keep this in a safe place.

Parting Comments

Well, that's that. You have now finished your spell as a conveyancing clerk. I hope that you enjoyed the experience. Perhaps you found some of the steps in the procedure quite challenging and rather demanding, but the remaining feeling will no doubt be one of satisfaction at your achievement. With due ceremony, you may now put your file of papers in some safe place (as they will most likely be required for future reference) and return this book to the shelf.

One final comment; having successfully dealt with the legal formalities of buying your house, if you ever come to sell it, you will find the procedure child's play by comparison.

Part III: Selling

9 Preliminary Matters

The first question you must ask yourself is, 'What do I have to offer?'. Is your property freehold or leasehold? If it is leasehold, we will need to know the approximate length of the term of years granted by the lease, and the rent.

In seeking to attract a buyer, there are two main options open to you; you can either advertise privately, or instruct an estate agent. You should certainly try the first option. A little research into property prices and a well phrased, informative advertisement can work wonders!

In showing prospective purchasers round the property, be frank and, needless to say, honest in answering any questions. Allow people to take their time and meet any (reasonable) requests they might make for carpets to be lifted, or furniture to be moved, etc.

If the initial negotiations result in a would-be buyer making an offer, ask for further information to enable you to determine whether or not it is likely to bear fruit. Can the person finance the purchase? Is he waiting to dispose of his present, highly unsaleable, property?

Where a suitable offer is made, although you may indicate a general willingness to proceed, your 'acceptance' must be on the clear basis that it is subject to a formal contract being prepared and entered into, ie, that it is 'subject to contract'. In the initial negotiations, use these words if you wish. But in any event, *do not sign anything* that indicates that you have, quite unconditionally, agreed to sell.

When you have agreed to go ahead with the sale to a particular person, ask for his full name and address, and also for the name and address of his solicitor, if he will be instructing one.

This book is only designed to assist the layman to handle a basic domestic conveyancing transaction. If you are wishing to act for yourself on a sale of property, it is assumed that you (and any other person owning jointly with you) are the undisputed legal owner(s) of the freehold or leasehold interest, that you are in possession, and that you are wishing to sell the whole of your interest with vacant possession to be given to the purchaser. If this is not the case, this book is not for you. Thus, you must not consider using this book in any of the following cases:

1 You are a personal representative of a deceased owner.

2 You are someone with an interest in a company which, in fact, owns the property.

3 You are merely selling part of a piece of land that you own.

4 You are wishing to retain some rights over, or interest in, the property after you have disposed of it.

5 The property is to be sold by auction.

In any situation out of the ordinary, you must seek expert assistance.

10 Securing a Buyer

General Considerations

This chapter is entitled '*Securing* a buyer' to emphasise the fact that, as yet, nothing has been secured. Either party can withdraw without obligation. Therefore, the actions you are now about to take have, as their objective, the making of a formal, legal agreement to buy and sell. As steps towards achieving this objective, you will be required to do two main things; prepare the draft contract, and answer the purchaser's preliminary enquiries.

A typical timetable of the events leading to exchange of contracts might be as follows.

Day 1 Agree, subject to contract, to sell.

Day 2 Write to the purchaser's solicitor confirming the arrangement.

Make necessary arrangements to obtain documents of title.

Day 5 Commence preparation of the draft contract.

Day 7 Submit draft contract to purchaser's solicitor.

Day 14 Receive preliminary enquiries.

Day 15 Return preliminary enquiries with replies.

Day 20 Receive draft contract approved.

Day 28 Receive purchaser's part of the contract duly signed.

Day 30 Exchange contracts.

You will notice from that timetable that you should first of all write to the purchaser's solicitor confirming the arrangements. This clearly only applies if the purchaser is instructing a solicitor. We will be assuming that your purchaser is legally represented. If he is not, you should simply read 'purchaser' for any reference to 'purchaser's solicitor', unless the context otherwise requires.

When writing to the purchaser's solicitor, make it clear that your agreement to sell is only informal. Give details of the property, the solicitor's client, and state that you have agreed 'subject to contract' (actually using those words) to sell your house at the agreed price. Inform the solicitor that you will be forwarding a draft contract for approval as soon as possible.

Obtaining Your Documents of Title

Before you can prepare the draft contract, you must see your documents of title, or a copy of them.

If you hold the property free from any mortgage or charge, the deeds should be in your possession or control.

If your house is subject to a mortgage, the lender will, in all probability, have retained custody of your deeds as security for the loan. They will not be released to you except in return for payment of the amount outstanding. This will only be on completion of your sale, so you must now take steps to obtain a copy of your title documents.

Write to the building society (or other lender) concerned, telling them that you have agreed to sell your house and shall be discharging the mortgage in due course. Ask for an approximate statement of the amount required to redeem the mortgage and request the building society to instruct their solicitor to supply you with an abstract of title as soon as possible. Tell the building society that if their solicitor discovers that your title is registered at the Land Registry, details of the title number and district Registry (together with, in the case of leasehold property, a copy of the lease) will suffice.

If the building society's solicitor sends you an abstract of title (thus indicating that your title is unregistered), you should take steps to obtain for yourself one copy of the conveyancing form, Land Charges Act K15. On the other hand, where you are told that your title is registered, you must obtain the following forms :

1 copy of Land Registry form A44 (Application for Office Copies of Documents);

1 copy of Land Registry form 201 (Authority to Inspect the Register).

These forms may be obtained for a few pence each from any branch of Oyez Stationery (for addresses, see page 153), or any law stationer. Alternatively, you may obtain form K15 or form A44 from any HMSO bookshop or agent.

When received, the form 201, or form K15, may be placed in your file for the time being, but in the case of registered land, form A44 must be completed as soon as possible. An example of a completed form A44 is given in Fig 12 on page 118.

The form should be addressed to the appropriate district Land Registry serving the area in which your house is situated as listed on the back of the form. In the next four boxes enter details of the county and district, title number, the address of the property, and full names of yourself and any other person owning jointly with you. You are going to need a complete copy of the Register so, in the next section, put the figure '1' in the circle alongside 'comprehensive set', and 'X' in the box immediately below that ('filed plan'). In the final section, put an X in the third box to indicate that you are the registered proprietor. The form should be signed (by yourself and any other co-proprietor), dated, and addressed. In the appropriate place on the tear-off slip at the bottom, put your name, address, and telephone number.

The completed form should be sent to the appropriate district Land Registry with your remittance for the fee payable (presently £2.25). This fee may be paid either by way of Land Registry fee stamps (obtainable from any Head Post Office) affixed to the form, or by postal order or cheque in favour of HM

Form A.44

Application for Office Copies of Documents

H.M. Land Registry

1. Please see notes overleaf.
2. The address box below is printed so that, if desired, the form can be enclosed in a standard window envelope. Please send this application to the proper office (see note 8)

> **FEES**
> Affix fee stamps in this space or above it (see note 1)

The Chief Land Registrar,
BLANKTOWN District Land Registry,
BLANKTOWN,
BLANKSHIRE.

> **FOR OFFICIAL USE ONLY**
> Pending applications

County and district (or London Borough)... ...	BLANKSHIRE, NEWTOWN.
Title number (a separate form should normally be used for each title)	BA 123456
Short description of property	1, MAIN STREET, NEWTOWN, BLANKSHIRE.
Full name(s) of the registered proprietor(s) (in block letters) ...	ALBERT VENDOR

I/~~We~~ apply for the following office copies and enclose the appropriate standard fee. I/~~We~~ undertake to pay such further fee (if any) as may be payable under paragraph XII of the Land Registration Fee Order 1970.

NOTE: Please specify in the circle against the appropriate item the NUMBER of copies required and place an X in the box that denotes the correct alternative.

◯ Register entries only (see note 2 overleaf)	◯ Filed plan only or ◯ Form 102 certificate only (see notes 3 and 4 overleaf)	◯ Document referred to on register Specify document .... (see note 6 overleaf)	① Comprehensive set including either ☒ Filed plan or ☐ Form 102 certificate (see note 5 overleaf)
Fee 20p	Fee 10p	Fee 25p per document	Fee 50p

☐ The written authority of the registered proprietor(s) (or his solicitors) to inspect the register accompanies this application.

☐ I/We act for the registered proprietor(s)

☒ I am the registered proprietor.

Signed *A.Vendor* .   Date 1.7.78.   Tel. No. Newtown 1234.

Address 1, Main Street, Newtown, Blankshire.   Reference –

ALBERT VENDOR,
1, MAIN STREET,
NEWTOWN, BLANKSHIRE.

This panel must be completed USING BLOCK LETTERS, and inserting the name and address to which the office copies are to be sent.

Applicant's reference –

Applicant's telephone no. Newtown 1234.

Fig 12

Land Registry. In a few days, you will receive facsimile copies of the entries on the Register.

With your title documents, or a copy of them in front of you, you must now 'investigate your title'.

Investigating your Title

Your immediate concern is to ascertain the precise legal quality of what you have to offer. You will do this by investigating your title, ie, carefully reading through your documents of title.

First, you must establish whether or not the title to your house is registered at HM Land Registry. If you hold the property subject to a mortgage, the building society's solicitor will have given you this information in response to your initial request and a copy of your documents of title will now be in your possession.

Where the originals of your title documents are in your possession, look through them, searching particularly for an HM Land Registry land certificate. This document is about 15 x 10in in size. Its buff cover has 'Land Certificate' printed on it and encloses a map showing your property and several pages of typed particulars. The presence of a land certificate means that title has been registered.

Where the examination of your original deeds reveals that your title is registered, you should now obtain for yourself an office copy of the entries on the official Register at HM Land Registry (and a copy of form 201) by following the procedure outlined in pages 117–119. If you have discovered that you own unregistered land, obtain instead one copy of Land Charges Act form K15.

You should now proceed to investigate your title in line with the principles set out under the heading 'Investigating the Vendor's Title' in Chapter 6 of this book (pages 52–68). In those pages, the procedure of investigating title is explained from the point of view of a purchaser. In your reading, you must bear this change of context in mind and make any necessary adjustments.

For example, at a particular point, a purchaser may be told

to raise a requisition on title to resolve some apparent difficulty. Such instructions are not addressed to you. Rather, you ought to be considering whether you could *answer* a requisition on such a matter if one were submitted to you. If you feel that you could, then there is no problem. However, if you discover something that amounts to a real defect in the chain of ownership which you cannot resolve, you must take legal advice.

Also, that explanation of investigating title is given on the basis that the purchaser merely has in his possession a copy of the owner's documents of title, and not the originals themselves. You will only be in this position if your house is subject to a mortgage. (Before you can consider selling your property, you must be sure that you or your building society is in possession of original deeds and documents sufficient to prove your ownership. Where the documents are in your possession, the comments on page 95 may prove helpful to you as you try to identify the originals.)

As he investigates title, the attention of a purchaser of unregistered land is drawn to the result of land charges searches made against the names of previous owners. He is instructed to consider the entries revealed by those searches, and is told that, if there does not appear to have been a search made against a particular name, then he must search against that name before he completes his purchase. Where you are selling property with unregistered title, you too must follow those instructions, except that any necessary search should be made now. Where the original title deeds are in your possession, the bundle of documents will include the certificates of result of previous land charge searches (forms K17 or K18, or the old form LC11). Where the deeds are in the possession of your building society, the abstract of title should contain details of all searches. To the list of any names to be searched against add the name of yourself and any co-owner. Using the K15 form, you should now make a search of the Land Charges Register in the manner described in pages 33–36.

You must consider the result of each search to determine whether any of the entries revealed affect the house that you own. Apply the comments in pages 36–41 to decide whether a particular entry does relate, and if so, its effect.

Where the registration does affect what you own, you will be subject to that charge. Thus, in relation to each relevant registered charge, you must be sure that, either it has already been cancelled (eg, previous mortgages), it is to be removed as part of your sale (eg, second mortgages granted by you, or class F charges), or that the contract for sale that you are preparing will indicate that the sale is to be subject to the charge (eg, restrictive covenants).

Where your title is registered, your investigation of title will consist of considering the entries on the Register. If you have the original land certificate in your possession, by all means conduct this examination by perusing that document, but also read through the office copy entries that you are obtaining since this will provide the most up-to-date indication of the state of the Register.

Whether the title is registered or unregistered, if the property is leasehold, you must remember that the lease forms the whole basis on which you occupy the house, and its terms must be strictly observed. Thus, your investigation of title must include a thorough reading of the lease, looking particularly for any terms which must be complied with in a sale of the property. Some leases stipulate that the licence of the landlord must be obtained. Such licence, or consent, must be obtained before contracts can be signed. In other cases, the lease may require notice of intended assignment to be given. You must make a note of any such requirement (and of the amount of the fee payable). You will have to give the notice before completion. (If the lease simply requires notice to be given after the assignment has taken place, this will be a matter for the purchaser to attend to after completion).

In the comments on investigating title, at certain points a purchaser is told that if he is faced with a particular situation, he must seek expert assistance. This is because the circumstances are such that, as a layman, he is not qualified to determine whether the document before him proves the vendor's ownership of the property concerned. You will clearly be in the same position and, where necessary, you must do the same. You cannot consider selling unless you know that you own your house, and, just as important, that you can prove your ownership.

Preparing the Draft Contract

Now that you have completed your investigation of title and have discovered just what you own, you are in a position to prepare a contract for its sale.

The contract must describe the property and set out the terms, or conditions, on which it will be sold.

You will find, set out in Fig 13 on pages 124 and 125, the skeleton around which you should prepare your contract. This outline incorporates the Statutory Form of Conditions of Sale, 1925 (a standard form setting out the usual conditions), a copy of which (official reference SR & O 1925/779) can be obtained for a few pence from any HMSO bookshop or law stationers.

Ultimately, the draft contract should be typed in duplicate (one and a carbon, to ensure that both parts are exactly the same) for submitting to the purchaser's solicitor for approval. However, before you attempt that task, you should be prepared to make at least one rough outline.

To prepare your draft contract, work through the specimen, completing the blanks in the manner described below.

Do not enter a date. This will be completed when contracts are signed and exchanged.

Alongside the words 'the Vendor', put the full name of yourself and any other person who owns the property jointly with you. The name(s) should agree with your name(s) as set out in the deed by which the property was conveyed to you, or as stated on the HM Land Registry Register. If the details in such documents are now inaccurate, eg, because of a subsequent change of name on marriage, the present name should be put in the contract. Following your name(s) as vendor(s), put your full address, and your occupation.

In the space provided for the description of the purchaser, insert the full name and address of the person who has offered to buy the house.

At the end of clause 1, enter the agreed purchase price in words and figures.

In clause 2 you are required to give a description of your property sufficient to identify it. If title to the property is registered, such a description may be given in simple terms as follows, eg, 'The property is the land and dwelling-house known as 1 Main Street Newtown Blankshire registered at HM Land Registry with absolute title [or, good leasehold title, as the case may be] under title number BA 123456'.

Where title is not registered, your house can conveniently be described by reference to the full description contained in the deed which transferred the house to you, for example :

The property is the semi-detached dwelling-house known as 1 Main Street Newtown Blankshire with the land forming the site thereof being more particularly described in a Conveyance dated the 10th April 1968 and made between John Williams Smith and Albert Vendor

One word of caution; if the description you are referring to is no longer correct, eg, because of boundary changes, make sure that you point out how the present description differs from the previous one so that the contract accurately describes what you are now able to dispose of.

The tenure of the property, ie, whether it is freehold or leasehold, should be entered to complete clause 3. Where the tenure is leasehold, make some reference to the lease (or underlease) and the term granted, eg, 'The tenure of the property is leasehold for a term of 999 years from the 1st January 1930 granted by a Lease dated the 1st January 1930 and made between Alan Brown and Charles Davies'.

You are obliged to give the purchaser details of all incumbrances that the property is being sold subject to, eg, restrictive covenants, rights of way, etc. Such matters, if any, should be referred to in clause 4. Your investigation of title will have discovered any such matters affecting your house which originate with the documents of title. They will have been contained, or referred to, in the various conveyances or, if the title is registered,

THIS AGREEMENT is made the   day of   19

Between the Vendor:

and the Purchaser:

1   The Vendor shall sell and the Purchaser shall buy in accordance
with the terms of this contract the property described herein at the
price of
(£   ).

2   The Property is

3   The tenure of the Property is

4   The Property is sold subject to all rights of way, water, light,
drainage, and other rights, easements, quasi-easements, privileges and
liabilities affecting the same

5   The Vendor sells as
6   Title shall be deduced

7   The date fixed for completion is   19
8   Vacant possession shall be given on completion.
9   The Purchaser shall pay a deposit of £10 per cent. of the purchase
price on the signing of this agreement.
10   The Purchaser buys the Property with full notice of its actual
state and condition and, where necessary, the conveyance to the
Purchaser shall modify any statutory covenant to be implied on the
part of the Vendor to exclude liability which would otherwise be
imposed on him in respect of such matters.

11   Where the Property is sold subject to any stipulation, covenant, or provision for breach or non-performance of which the Vendor or his estate will remain liable after conveyance then, save to the extent that a covenant for indemnity will be implied under section 77 of the Law of Property Act, 1925 or section 24 of the Land Registration Act, 1925, the Purchaser shall in the conveyance to him covenant to observe and perform the same and to indemnify the Vendor and his estate against all actions and claims in respect thereof.

12   Where the parts of this contract are exchanged through the post, the contract is made when the last part is posted.

13   The Property is sold subject to the Statutory Form of Conditions of Sale, 1925 so far as those conditions are not inconsistent with any of the provisions of this contract and subject to the following particular amendments:-

    (a)   completion shall take place at such office or place as the Vendor shall reasonably require;

    (b)   the rate of interest under condition 4 shall be £15 per cent. per annum;

    (c)   time shall be deemed to be of the essence for the purposes of condition 6.

Signed

    Vendor (who also hereby acknowledges receipt of a deposit of £   ):

    Purchaser:

Fig 13

in the Charges Register of the title. In cases where the matters are mentioned in the documents of title, you have done your duty if you direct the purchaser to the relevant document. Thus, in an unregistered transaction, to complete this part of the contract you might add to the end of clause 4, '. . . and to the covenants and other provisions contained mentioned or referred to in a [or, the said] Conveyance dated . . .'.

If title to the property is registered and the only entry on the Charges Register is in respect of your present mortgage, there is no need to make any addition to clause 4 since you will not be selling the property subject to that charge. It will be paid off as part of the sale. (If this is not your intention, you should not be using this book. Seek legal advice.)

Where there are matters other than a mortgage referred to in the Charges Register, it will be necessary to mention these in the contract. This might be done as follows, '. . . and to the matters noted on the Charges Register at HM Land Registry'. If the Charges Register also refers to a mortgage which is to be discharged add, 'with the exception of the entry(ies) numbered . . . thereon'. In this way it will be clear that the purchaser is not being expected to buy subject to this.

It could be that, as owner of the property, you are subject to some positive obligation to perform some act, eg, to construct a fence, as referred to on the Proprietorship Register. Should it be your desire to pass that obligation to the purchaser, the words you add to clause 4 of the contract should make it clear that the property is being sold subject to it, eg, 'and to the covenant(s) referred to in the Proprietorship Register'.

Whether your title is registered or unregistered, be sure to phrase your additions to clause 4 of the contract in terms sufficiently wide to include all matters that you are selling the property subject to. Where the property is leasehold, state that the property is subject 'to the tenant's covenants and the conditions contained in the Lease and to the payment of the [eg, yearly] rent of £...... thereby reserved'.

Should you experience any difficulty in seeking to complete clause 4, you will have to take legal advice.

In clause 5 you are required to specify the capacity in which you sell the property. If you are a sole legal owner entitled to the property for your own benefit, you should indicate that you sell as 'beneficial owner'. If you and some other person(s) are joint legal owners, the appropriate description is 'trustees'. If you do not fall into either of these two categories, you must place the matter in expert hands.

The words necessary to complete clause 6 vary as to whether the property has registered or unregistered title.

Where you are selling property with registered title, clause 6 should be completed by the addition of the words, 'in accordance with section 110 Land Registration Act, 1925'.

Where title is not registered, you are required to specify in clause 6 the document which will be the starting point in the chain of ownership that you will show, or deduce, to the purchaser. Working back down the chain of ownership leading to you, go to a point fifteen years ago. Now look at the first deed before that date which disposed of the property, eg, a conveyance, or assignment. Provided that this document describes or identifies the property adequately, it may be used as your starting point. If it does not, work farther back down the chain until a suitable document is located.

Where the property is leasehold, not only must you show title back to the first assignment that is at least fifteen years old, but you must also provide the purchaser with a copy of the lease.

If the deed you propose to use refers to a plan or covenants contained in an earlier document, it will be necessary to supply the purchaser with a copy of the earlier material.

Thus, in the case of unregistered freehold property, clause 6 of the contract might be completed as follows, 'and shall commence with a Conveyance dated the 1st June 1960 and made between Beautiful Builders Company Limited and John Williams Smith'. Where the property is leasehold, an appropriate entry might be, 'and shall commence with the Lease and continue with an Assignment dated 1st October 1958 and made between George Harrison and Ian Jenkins'.

When you have reached this far in the contract, you have, so to speak, completed all the blanks, and you need now only include the remaining clauses just as they are set out for you in the specimen. In clause 7, leave the completion date blank. It will be inserted on exchange of contracts. Note that, by clause 8, you undertake to give the purchaser vacant possession of the property on completion.

It will probably not be possible to type all of the contract on one side of a sheet of paper. Rather than continuing to type on a separate sheet, which could easily become separated from its companion, type the remaining portion of the contract on the reverse side of the paper.

Documents to Accompany the Draft Contract

The nature of the documents that you will be sending with the contract will depend upon whether your title is registered or not.

(a) Property with Unregistered title—In unregistered conveyancing, you will be giving the purchaser an abstract of title. This consists of copies (photographic, or typed) of the deeds and documents that show a chain of ownership leading to you.

If you hold the property subject to a mortgage, the building society's solicitor will have supplied you with an abstract of title. This can now be passed on to the purchaser. However, if the building society's solicitor sent you a 'marked' abstract, ie, one which bears the actual markings of a solicitor that it has been compared against the original deeds, it may be the only evidence that you have of the events there related. Hence, that original marked abstract must not be given to the purchaser. Let him have a photocopy of it.

Where your house is not subject to a mortgage but the original deeds are in your possession, you must prepare your own abstract of title by having copies made of all the documents that constitute the chain of ownership leading to you, starting with the document specified in clause 6 of the contract. Include any mortgages and the vacating receipts endorsed on them. With the deeds, you will no doubt have certificates of result of land charges searches that have been made by previous purchasers (either on the old land charges from LC 11, or on the modern forms K17 or K18). Copy these too.

(b) Property with registered title—Now that you have, as part of the process of investigating your title, examined the office copy of the entries on the Register at HM Land Registry that you obtained some days ago, it is of no further use to you and can be passed to the purchaser's solicitor.

If the Register is not complete in itself but refers to matters set out in some other document, eg, the covenants contained in a particular deed, the purchaser must also be supplied with a copy of that document. The lease, in the case of leasehold property, clearly falls into this category.

Submitting the Draft Contract for Approval

The draft contract, in duplicate, and the documents which must accompany it, should be posted to the purchaser's solicitor for his approval. However, before you do so, delete from the abstract, or office copies, all reference to the price that you paid for the property when you bought. If the buyer discovers what that was, he may decide that his offer is too generous and withdraw it.

Where your title is registered, the price that you paid might appear in the remarks column next to your name in the Proprietorship Register. Cut it out. If the office copy entries happen to include a copy of your purchase deed, delete from it any reference to the price, or consideration (see below).

In the case of unregistered title, to remove any indication of the price you paid for the house, you should cut from the copy of the deed (*not* the original, of course) transferring the property to you the words which state the consideration for that disposition (this may appear not only at the start of the operative part of the deed, but also in the recitals). The certificate of value clause (if any) can sometimes give an indication of the price being paid and, if necessary, the amount of the certificate should be deleted. Further, if stamp duty was paid, cut the images of the Inland Revenue stamps from the copy of the deed.

When contracts are eventually exchanged you will have to supply this deleted information to the purchaser, but at that time it will cause no harm.

Although your letter will say that the contract is enclosed 'for approval', this phrase is used more as a matter of courtesy than as a serious invitation to suggest amendments. It is your privilege to decide on the terms of the sale. The purchaser's solicitor may suggest some addition to the contract to cover a matter that he feels ought to be dealt with formally, eg, a clause providing for the transfer to his client of your rights under any NHBC Agreement and Protection Certificate. When this happens, you will no doubt be prepared to consider, and accept, any reasonable suggestions. However, so far as the set conditions of sale are concerned, they are perfectly fair and reasonable and should require no alteration.

In relation to clause 9 of the contract, the purchaser's solicitor may suggest that it be amended so as to provide that the deposit shall be paid to a third person. Do not entertain such a suggestion. The house is yours, and there is no reason at all why you should not be paid a deposit. If you are involved in a simultaneous sale and purchase, you will no doubt be wanting to use the deposit you receive on the sale as the deposit on your purchase. Should you agree to the sale deposit being paid to a stakeholder, you will not be able to do this.

Where you are prepared to accept some addition to the draft contract, care should be taken to ensure that both parts of the contract are amended in exactly the same way.

Answering the Preliminary Enquiries

As soon as the purchaser's solicitor has looked through the draft contract he will submit preliminary enquiries to resolve any queries raised thereby and to elicit information on more general matters concerning the property, eg, ownership of walls and fences, services available, etc.

The preliminary enquiries will be submitted in duplicate, the copy being sent for your use. Most likely a standard printed form will be used which sets out the questions on the left-hand side of the page with space on the right for the answers.

All your answers to the preliminary enquiries must be candid, and scrupulously truthful. Do not try to mislead the purchaser with half-truths. If you do not know the answer to a particular enquiry, eg, who owns the boundary fences, say so. Do not guess at the meaning of a question and make what you hope will be a suitable reply. If necessary, ask the purchaser's solicitor what the enquiry is about.

The purchaser will probably ask whether the house is covered by the NHBC protection scheme, and if so, he may request a copy of the Agreement, and certificate. (Do not hand over the original of any such document except on formal completion of the sale.)

One of the matters that the purchaser will be particularly concerned about is whether or not the property is affected by any adverse rights in favour of third parties, eg, rights of way, drainage, etc. In reply, disclose *all* such rights known to you. (In registered conveyancing, these rights of third parties come under the heading of overriding interests, ie, interests which bind a purchaser even though they are not specifically referred to on the Register.) There is no need to disclose any such rights if they are apparent on inspection, eg, telephone wires passing over the property, or are specifically described in the draft contract.

You are quite likely to be asked to confirm that all fixtures and fittings are included in the sale. If you intend to remove a particular fixture, you must draw this to the attention of the purchaser. Where an item is to be included in the sale, it must be yours. Any hire-purchase account will have to be settled before completion.

Write, or type your replies on both copies of the form. The top copy should be returned to the purchaser's solicitor with a covering letter.

Purchaser's Approval of the Contract

In due course, the purchaser's solicitor will notify you of his approval of the terms of the contract and return one copy of it to you.

This approval may be given even though the purchaser is still waiting for his financial arrangements to be finalised. Sometimes the purchaser's solicitor prefers to withhold the approval of the draft contract until his client has actually signed his part of it, when the approved contract for your use will accompany the purchaser's signed contract.

When you receive the contract approved, check that any alterations or amendments that were agreed have been correctly made.

Although the contract which you prepared was called the 'draft' contract, the two parts may be used as the formal documents to be signed by yourself and the purchaser, unless there are considerable amendments that render them unsuitable. If the draft cannot be used, it is your responsibility to prepare fresh contracts for signature.

Completion Date

It is essential that you *do not sign the contract* unless it has had a completion date, ie, a date when the purchaser will pay his money and you will give possession, inserted in clause 7. This date should be arranged to suit both yourself and the purchaser. Allow one month or so from exchange of contracts for the purchaser to attend to the pre-completion legal formalities. Where you are involved in a simultaneous sale and purchase, the completion date for your sale must tie in with your purchase.

It may be that the purchaser is reluctant to commit himself on a completion date, perhaps because he is unsure as to when the sale of his own house will be completed. Although you may appreciate his difficulties, press for agreement on a completion date and exchange of contracts. If no better arrangements are forthcoming, you may be prepared to exchange contracts on the basis of a firm completion date several months hence.

Exchange of Contracts

When you receive the purchaser's part of the contract duly signed, together with the deposit, stop and ask yourself, 'Am I ready to exchange contracts?'

It is most important that you give careful thought to this question now since, once contracts are exchanged, you will be legally bound to sell. It will be too late to change your mind. Thus, before you make any move, make sure that you have agreed a completion date and, if you are involved in a simultaneous sale and purchase, that you have considered the comments on pages 149 and 150.

To exchange contracts, insert the agreed completion date in clause 7 of your part of the contract (and in the purchaser's signed contract if this has not been done already). You and any other person who owns the property jointly with you, should sign your part of the contract in the space provided, and insert the amount of the deposit that you have received. Finally, date both parts of the contract at the top of the first page.

To make the arrangement legally binding, write to the purchaser's solicitor enclosing the part of the contract that you have signed.

Where your title is registered, your part of the contract should be accompanied by the completed form 201, Authority to Inspect the Register. At the top of the form, enter details of the county and district, title number, and postal address of your property. In the box below the heading, put the name and address of yourself and any other co-proprietor. Delete the words, 'as solicitor for . . . of . . .' that follow. In the space after the words, 'hereby authorise Messrs . . .' put the name and address of the purchaser's solicitor (or the purchaser personally, if he is not represented). The form should be signed by yourself and any other co-proprietor, and dated.

If the Purchaser does not Agree to Buy

It is not in every case that the person to whom a draft contract is submitted will actually sign a contract and agree to buy. Not being legally bound to purchase, he is perfectly entitled to withdraw (as you are, of course).

If your purchaser does back out, write to his solicitor and ask him to return the draft contract and contract documents that you submitted to him. When this has actually been done, any preliminary deposit paid by the purchaser that you hold may be returned.

A purchaser has no right to withdraw once the two parts of the contract have been exchanged. Clause 12 of your contract provides that a legal agreement is made at the time your part is posted. From that time onward, the purchaser cannot simply change his mind and back out of the transaction. Should your purchaser suggest that this is his intention, you should warn him that, if he does not proceed, you will take legal action. If it turns out to be necessary, you must carry out your threat.

11 Before Completion

General considerations

A typical timetable of events from contract to completion is given below.

Day 1 Contracts exchanged.

Day 10 Requisitions on title received from purchaser's solicitor together with draft purchase deed for approval.

Day 13 Replies given to requisitions on title and draft deed returned approved.

Day 17 Purchase deed received from purchaser's solicitor ready for completion.

Day 20 Completion statement prepared and sent to purchaser's solicitor.

Day 27 Completion arrangements made.

Day 30 Completion.

It is only on completion, when the purchase money has been paid, that the purchaser is entitled to possession of the property. *Under no circumstances should you allow the purchaser to take possession of your house until he has paid the agreed price in full.* You have been warned!

Before completion, you will need to make the necessary removal arrangements. On completion, the house should be empty, though the purchaser may be prepared to allow you a few hours to actually move out once the sale has been completed.

Where your property is subject to a mortgage, as soon as contracts have been exchanged you should write to the building society's solicitor giving him details of the agreed completion date and requesting a detailed statement of the amount required to discharge the mortgage at that time (and the daily interest figure to enable you to calculate the up-to-date redemption figure should completion be delayed for a few days).

If your property is leasehold, the terms of the lease may require you to give the landlord notice of your intention to assign. In such cases, write to the person (or firm) to whom the rent is payable, giving details of the property and the lease and stating that you intend to assign to the purchaser (supplying his name and address). Include your remittance for any fee payable. Send a carbon copy with the letter and ask for the duplicate to be returned, receipted.

Answering the Purchaser's Requisitions on Title

Once contracts have been exchanged, the purchaser will set about investigating your title to the property. He will seek to resolve any difficulties by appropriate requisitions on title. You will receive requisitions on title in duplicate, most likely in the same format as the preliminary enquiries.

As with your replies to the preliminary enquiries, what you say in answer to the requisitions on title should be frank, open and honest.

The purchaser will most likely stipulate that, on completion, the last receipts for general rates, and other outgoings (eg, ground rent, in the case of leasehold property) must be produced. Your reply should be 'agreed'. Between now and completion you must contact the local authority and notify them of the forthcoming change of ownership. Arrange to pay your share of the year's rates bill (or to make any necessary claim for sums overpaid). Take similar action in relation to water charges.

A requisition is sure to be raised concerning the title deeds of the property. If your title is not registered, the purchaser will wish you to confirm that the originals of all the abstracted deeds and documents will be handed over on completion. Where you are now selling only part of the land comprised in the first link in the chain, it may be that your only evidence of part of the chain of ownership is a marked abstract of title. Where this is the case, you will have to detail those original deeds which will not be handed over, and give the name of the person who sold part and gave the acknowledgement. If the deeds are in the possession of your building society's solicitor, he will be able to supply the necessary information.

Where your title is registered, the purchaser will want confirmation that the original land/charge certificate will be handed over on completion. He may also wish to know the date on which the certificate was brought up to date with the Register itself. This date is stamped on the inside of the front cover. If the certificate is in the possession of your building society's solicitor, he will be able to tell you the date.

In the case of leasehold property, you will be required to hand over the original lease (or a marked abstract and an acknowledgement for production) on completion.

The purchaser will require you to confirm that all subsisting mortgages will be discharged on or before completion. Strictly speaking, before the purchaser is obliged to pay his money, he must be given some evidence to show that existing mortgages have been repaid. Normally though, a building society will only seal a vacating receipt (or Land Registry discharge form) when it actually receives payment of the outstanding balance. Since you are probably intending to pay off the mortgage with the money the purchaser will give you on completion, this causes something of a difficulty.

However, the problem will be overcome if the purchaser's solicitor is prepared to accept an undertaking from your building society's solicitor to forward the sealed discharge document as soon as it is available. Thus, in your reply to the requisition, you could indicate that such an undertaking will be given.

If the purchaser insists that the sealed vacating receipt (or discharge) must actually be available on completion, you must be prepared to meet his demands.

Should it be that the building society's solicitor states that his client will not seal the document until the money is actually received, you will have to arrange for the balance outstanding to be repaid before completion. Your bank will probably be prepared to give you a short-term loan for this purpose. The bank will normally want the building society's solicitor to undertake to hand your deeds to them when the mortgage has been discharged and this will mean that completion will take place at the bank. Do not make any such arrangements for the early discharge of your mortgage until after the purchaser has received, and accepted, your replies to his requisitions on title.

In response to a requisition requesting a statement of the amount due on completion, reply, 'to follow'. (We will be dealing with this aspect of the procedure very shortly.)

Besides standard requisitions on title such as are discussed above, the purchaser's solicitor may raise requisitions on specific problems concerning your claim to ownership. Deal with these as best you can. If you do not understand the question, discuss the matter with the purchaser's solicitor. Your building society's solicitor may be able to assist you to formulate suitable replies. If you encounter insurmountable difficulties, you will have to seek expert assistance.

The replies to the requisitions should be written, or typed, on both copies of the form. The carbon copy is for your use. Date both forms, and sign the top copy. This should be returned to the purchaser's solicitor.

Should it be that your replies to the requisitions do not satisfy the purchaser's solicitor and there is some major point of controversy between you which cannot be resolved and which threatens to cause the collapse of the sale, you will have to take legal advice.

The purchaser's solicitor investigated your title to the property by looking through the copy documents that you sent to him. Before he pays the purchase money, he will want to compare those copies against the originals. Usually, this is the first thing that the purchaser's solicitor does on completion. Some solicitors prefer to verify the copy documents as soon as the requisitions have been answered. Be prepared to grant this facility. If the original documents are in the possession of your building society's solicitor, you will have to make arrangements for the purchaser's solicitor to examine them there.

Approving the Draft Purchase Deed

When you receive the draft purchase deed from the purchaser's solicitor, it is for you to decide whether or not you are prepared to execute a document in that form so as to make the purchaser the owner of your house. The purchase deed must accord with the terms of the contract. Thus, your main concern is to be sure that the details of it (eg, parties, price, property, etc) are accurate, and that you are not being asked to convey more, or on different terms, than you have contracted to convey.

To familiarise yourself with what you should be looking for, you should read pages 70–78 of this book, where it is explained, from a purchaser's point of view, how to prepare the draft purchase deed. Remember though, that the form of deed suggested there is not necessarily the form that your purchaser will choose. Rather than concentrating on the style there discussed, consider what the various parts of the deed achieve. Provided your purchaser's deed is accurate and effective, it can be approved.

If there are any features of the purchase deed that you are unhappy with, telephone the purchaser's solicitor and discuss the matter with him. He may agree that some alteration is necessary, and the two of you will be able to settle the precise terms of any amendment. Where it is not possible for you to reach agreement, you will have to seek legal advice.

When you are happy with the form of the draft purchase deed, write to the purchaser's solicitor returning the top copy of the draft, and stating that you approve it, either as drawn, or with the suggested amendments. The carbon copy of the purchase deed, completed with any corrections and amendments, should be placed in your file.

Preparing the Completion Statement

You must now prepare an account, or statement, giving details of the amount due from the purchaser on completion, and showing how this figure has been arrived at.

The starting figure is obviously the agreed purchase price. Against this, the purchaser must be given credit for any deposit he has paid. In some cases, that will be all the completion statement contains. In other cases, the statement may need to refer to ground rent, and the price of furniture and fittings included in the sale.

Unless the change of ownership is to take place on a rent payment date, where you are selling leasehold property (or freehold property subject to a chief rent) the demand for the current rent period will have to be apportioned on a daily basis between yourself and the purchaser. To make this apportionment you will need to look at the lease (or a copy of it) to ascertain how the rent is payable, whether yearly or half-yearly, in advance or in arrear. (If you hold the property subject to a mortgage, and you have parted with your only copy of the lease to the purchaser, you will have to ask the building society's solicitor for such details.) Most ground rents are payable in arrear and any apportionment will result in an allowance to the purchaser.

Except in cases where the rent owner will know of the change in ownership of your house (eg, by his being given notice under the terms of the lease) you should write to the person to whom rent is paid notifying him of the forthcoming sale, giving the full name of the purchaser, and requesting that all future demands be addressed to him.

You must also take steps to obtain a final account for the gas, electricity and telephone, and request the authority concerned to direct all future accounts to the purchaser.

If you agreed to sell some items of furniture or furnishings for a price in addition to the purchase price for the house, the completion statement will need to include the agreed sum.

Having decided how much is due from the purchaser on completion, you must now consider how you wish that money to be paid to you.

In the absence of anything to the contrary being agreed, the purchaser will pay the balance due on completion by a banker's draft in your favour. A banker's draft is basically a cheque drawn by a bank on itself. If your house is subject to a mortgage, you will no doubt want some of the purchase price to go to pay off that mortgage (or, if this is being discharged in advance of completion by your bank, to repay the bank loan). Thus you will need two banker's drafts, one in favour of your building society (which can immediately be passed on to repay the loan), and one for the balance in your favour. So, where you do have a mortgage, you must contact the building society's solicitor to ascertain the precise amount required to pay off the mortgage (if you have not been told this already), and in whose favour the banker's draft should be drawn.

Where you are involved in a simultaneous sale and purchase, your requirements in the way of banker's drafts will have to take into account the fact that, not only will you be wanting to pay off a mortgage, but also that you will probably wish to use the remainder of the sale price immediately as part of the purchase price on your new house. If you are involved in a chain transaction, you are referred to pages 151 and 152 of this book.

When the completion statement has been worked out, it should be typed (with a carbon copy for your file) and sent to the purchaser's solicitor with details of how payment is to be made.

Executing the Purchase Deed

When you receive the engrossment of the purchase deed, check it, word for word, against the draft approved by you. If there are discrepancies, the engrossment should be returned to the purchaser's solicitor for correction.

If the purchase deed contains covenants, ie, promises, by the purchaser(s), it must have been signed, sealed and delivered by him (them). In the absence of any covenants, the purchaser(s) need not execute the deed, but usually will. Sealing is indicated by a red wafer seal stuck to the deed alongside the signature. Where a deed which should have been signed, sealed and delivered by the purchaser has not been so executed, it must be returned to the purchaser's solicitor.

The manner of executing a deed is explained on page 83. Following the instructions there given, you and any other co-vendor should execute the deed transferring ownership to the purchaser. Do not date the deed. This will be done later. The executed deed should be placed in your file to await completion.

Preparing for Completion

About four or five days or so before completion is due, you should make the detailed preparation described below.

(a) Where and when? If you hold your house subject to a mortgage, completion will have to take place at the offices of your building society's solicitor. (Where your mortgage was paid off in advance of completion with a loan from your bank, they may have stipulated a particular venue.) You will need to attend at that place in person. If there are other persons who own the house jointly with you, it is not necessary for them to attend on completion provided they have executed the purchase deed in advance. In cases where there is no mortgage and the original title documents are in your possession, you may choose the venue for completion. You may already have given the purchaser's solicitor some indication as to where you would like to complete.

The actual date and time of completion should be fixed to suit all concerned (do not forget your building society's solicitor!). Remember, if you are involved in a simultaneous sale and purchase, any arrangements now being made on your sale must be compatible with those being considered for your purchase. Where you are involved in a chain transaction, you are referred to Chapter 15 of this book.

If the purchaser's solicitor indicates that he will not be ready to complete on the date specified in the contract, your only remedy for delay of only a few days or so is to charge the purchaser interest on the balance of the purchase money at the rate specified in clause 13(b) of the contract (£15 per cent per annum). Such interest should be calculated on a daily basis from the contractual completion date to the actual completion date, and added to the balance due as shown in the completion statement. If it is anticipated that the delay will extend beyond a few days, you should seek legal advice as to the steps you might take to compel completion.

(b) What to do? The first thing that the purchaser will want to do on completion (unless he has done it beforehand) is compare his copies of your documents of title with the originals. These should therefore be collected together and a list of them prepared (in duplicate). On completion, ask the purchaser's solicitor to sign one copy of the list by way of receipt. (If you hold your property subject to a mortgage and the original documents of title are in the possession of the solicitor acting for your building society, you will not have this task of getting the documents ready for completion.)

Where your property is subject to a mortgage, your building society's solicitor will release your documents of title on completion when he receives the amount owing under the mortgage. At the same time, he will give you the mortgage deed with a vacating receipt endorsed on it, duly sealed by the lender (or, in the case of registered land, will hand you a sealed form of discharge, form 53). Alternatively, if the purchaser's solicitor has indicated a willingness to accept such, the building society's solicitor will give his written undertaking to forward the discharge document to the purchaser's solicitor as soon as possible.

When you obtained your loan from the building society, you may have assigned the benefit of an insurance policy as additional security. If this was the case with you, you must make a point of ensuring that neither the policy, nor the deed of assignment relating to it, is handed to the purchaser on completion. In rare cases the one deed may have been used both as the mortgage deed and also as the deed of assignment of the policy. If this happens to be the way that your mortgage and assignment of policy was prepared (if necessary, inquire of the building society's solicitor), you must contact the insurance company concerned in advance of completion to ascertain what they wish you to do in these circumstances, and, if necessary, obtain expert assistance.

Beside examining and collecting your title deeds and documents, the purchaser's solicitor will require you to hand over the executed purchase deed. Make sure that you have this ready, properly executed by yourself and any co-vendor, and witnessed.

Before the purchaser pays his price, he will wish to examine the last receipt for general rates and water rates, and, in the case of leasehold property, the last ground rent receipt. Where the terms of your lease are such that you were required to obtain the landlord's consent to the sale, or to give notice of intended assignment, the licence, or a receipted copy notice, must be available to be handed over on completion.

You may have agreed to give the purchaser some other document on completion, eg, NHBC certificate, and agreement. If so, they must be available. Where you have agreed to assign the benefit of your House Purchaser's Agreement, you will no doubt have been given a form of assignment for you to sign. This too must be handed over on completion.

By his requisitions on title, the purchaser's solicitor may have made some stipulation as to particular evidence of ownership, or documents relating to your house, which must be produced on completion. You must be ready to meet any such requirement.

The final matter to be considered in your preparation for completion is how the purchaser is to obtain possession of your house once he has paid for it. He may be prepared to allow you a few hours to actually vacate the property, but, on completion, he will want to be sure that adequate arrangements have been made whereby he will be given vacant possession. Such arrangements may have been made at the requisition on title stage. Perhaps the keys, or a set of them, can be handed over on completion. The balance of the keys (if any) could then be left on the property when you leave. Where the house was sold through an estate agent and he has a set of keys, you could telephone the agent on completion and authorise their release. Whatever arrangements you are considering must have the approval of the purchaser (or his solicitor).

So prepared, you are ready for completion.

12 Completion and After

On completion, the purchaser's solicitor will take the initiative to obtain everything he requires.

When the balance of the purchase money is offered to you, check that all banker's drafts are properly signed, for the correct amounts, and in favour of the right person(s). Do not accept payment by ordinary cheque. Where some of the money is to pay off an existing mortgage, the appropriate draft should be handed to your building society's solicitor. In return for this, he will release your title documents.

When the price has been paid, hand all your documents of title to the purchaser. Date the executed purchase deed with the date of completion, and complete your draft copy. Give the completed purchase deed to the purchaser. Finally, hand over the keys.

And that's that. House sold! All that remains is to cancel any insurance that you had on the property, and pay the estate agent (if any) his commission. That done, your file can be put away for future reference.

Well, how did you enjoy your spell as a conveyancer? I trust that you found the experience rewarding. One thing can be said for sure. Next time around, you will find the procedure even easier!

Part IV: Simultaneous Selling and Buying (The 'Chain')

13 The Problems of the 'Chain'

You are involved in a chain if you are selling one house and simultaneously buying another, and the two transactions cannot proceed *totally independently* of each other. Thus, this part of the book will be of concern to you, not only where you need the proceeds from your sale to pay for your purchase, but also where the purchase is being financed by a mortgage loan which will not be released until your existing mortgage is discharged (such a condition is often imposed by a building society).

The problems of the chain are self-evident. You cannot commit yourself to buy until you are sure that your buyer is committed to purchase. Thus, exchange of contracts must be synchronised. Further, the arrangements for completion must take account of the fact that you will not be able to buy until you receive the money on the sale. These two specific problems are dealt with in detail in Chapters 14 and 15 of this book.

There are, however, other general matters that should be borne in mind when embarking upon a chain transaction. It is clearly most important that you are sure of your finances. You should make an initial calculation to determine approximately how much money you will have available. You will need to take into account the amount necessary to redeem any existing mortgage on your present house, any sums which are to be deducted from the building society advance in respect of your new home, eg, the building society's solicitor's charges, and any stamp duty or HM Land Registry fees that will be payable.

When the two transactions are under way, apply Part II of this book to the purchase, and Part III to the sale, doing so quite independently. At the points where the two transactions must be co-ordinated, you will be directed to this part of the book. As you deal with the conveyancing work, keep all the papers and copy letters relative to the two sides of the chain in separate files.

14 Exchanging Contracts

In the chain transaction, the ideal arrangement is for contracts to be exchanged on the sale and purchase at the same time with all the parties involved being personally present. Because of the practical difficulties involved in making such arrangements, it is usual for exchange of contracts to be effected through the post. This procedure is quite satisfactory in most cases, but, because of the inevitable time-lag, there is always the possibility (though admittedly a very, very slight one) that one side of the chain will collapse, ie, that one person will change his mind and decide not to sell or buy. If it is the vendor of your new house who changes his mind after you have exchanged contracts on your sale, you will be left with no house. However, that risk is there whether you are being your own conveyancer or are legally represented. But, since your purchase is dependent upon your sale, you *must* first of all make your purchaser legally obliged to buy before you can consider committing yourself on your new house.

The *strict* procedure which you *must* adhere to when exchanging contracts is as follows. When you receive the purchaser's signed contract on the sale of your present house, exchange contracts with him as instructed in pages 132 and 133. As soon as you know that your part of the sale contract has actually been received by the purchaser's solicitor you may exchange contracts on your purchase, in the manner described in pages 47 and 48.

A 10 per cent deposit will most likely be payable on the signing of your contract to buy. For this purpose you will no doubt wish to use the money you received as the deposit on your sale. (You can only do this, of course, if the deposit has actually been paid to you, or to some other person as your agent, otherwise you will have to borrow the amount needed.) Should it be that the deposit on your sale is not sufficient to be a full 10 per cent deposit on your purchase, you may find that the solicitor acting for your vendor will be prepared to advise the acceptance of a smaller deposit.

15 Completing

Having regard to the fact that, on completion, you are obliged to give vacant possession to the purchaser of your present house, the order of completing the two sides of the chain transaction should be purchase first (to enable you to move out of your present house), then sale. However, since the money for your purchase is to come from your sale, you must first sell. In practice, this vicious circle is usually broken by the purchaser allowing the vendor a short time within which to complete the purchase of his new house and move. If the purchaser of your present house is not prepared to extend this concession to you, you must be ready to give him vacant possession on completion, as is his right. This may mean that you will need to arrange temporary accommodation for your family and yourself. (Removal vans are quite comfortable!)

The points mentioned above must be borne in mind as you consider your completion arrangements. It is usually most convenient for the two completions to follow each other as closely as possible, sale first, then purchase, perhaps both early on the day on which you will actually be moving out, or late in the afternoon of the day before your removals are due.

The purpose of completing your sale first is so that you will be able to proceed with your purchase. If you are to do this, the money on your sale must be paid to you in such form that it can be used straight away as part of the purchase price on your new house.

In a single sale transaction, if you hold your present house subject to a mortgage, you would arrange for part of the proceeds of sale to be paid to you by a banker's draft in favour of your building society. In the chain transaction, such arrangements are unchanged. However, in a chain transaction, you will also need to arrange for what is left of the proceeds of sale (after any mortgage has been discharged) to be paid to you in the form of a banker's draft in favour of the solicitor acting for the vendor of your new house (and his building society, if any, to pay off his existing mortgage). Where you are buying with the aid of a mortgage, you will be able to put with this banker's draft the draft that you will be receiving in respect of the advance. If the net mortgage advance and the surplus on your sale exceed what you will be required to pay on completion of your purchase, you will want the solicitor acting for the buyer of your present house to pay the amount of the excess by a banker's draft in your favour.

When you have worked out what your requirements are, give the appropriate instructions to the solicitor acting for the purchaser of your present house, and to the solicitor acting for the building society that is making an advance to assist you with the purchase of your new house.

Appendix A

Useful Addresses

Branches of Oyez Stationery Ltd
Birmingham : 55/59 Newhall Street, B3 3RF
Bristol : Room 1, The Guildhall, Bristol BS1 2HL
Cardiff : 31 Charles Street, Cardiff CF1 4EA
Leeds : 1 Albion Place, Leeds LS1 6JL
Liverpool : 41 North John Street, L2 5RF
London : 191/192 Fleet Street, EC4A 2JA; 15 Hanover Street, W1R 9HG; 49 Bedford Row, WC1R 4LS; 4 Broad Street Place, EC2M 7JY
Manchester : 28/30 John Dalton Street, M2 6HR
Newcastle-upon-Tyne : 1 & 2 Collingwood Buildings, Collingwood Street, Newcastle-upon-Tyne.
Sheffield : 7 Campo Lane, Sheffield S1 2EF
Southampton : 21 The Avenue, Southampton SO1 2SQ

Inland Revenue Stamp Offices
Birmingham : Stamp Office, First Floor, Edmund House, 12–22 Newhall Street, Birmingham B3 3DU
Bristol : Stamp Office, First Floor, Pithay House, All Saints Street, Bristol BS1 2NY
Cardiff : Companies House, Crown Way, Cardiff CF4 3UR
Leeds : Stamp Office, 42 Eastgate, Leeds LS2 7LD
Liverpool : Stamp Office, Tower Building, Water Street, Liverpool L3 1AE
London : (Head Office) The Controller of Stamps, Inland Revenue, Bush House, South-West Wing, Strand, London WC2B 4QN; (City Office) Stamp Office, 61 Moorgate, London EC2R 6BH; (Stock Exchange) Stamp Office, 26 Austin Friars, London EC2N 2EH

Manchester : Stamp Office, Albert Bridge House, Bridge Street, Manchester M60 9BT

Newcastle-upon-Tyne : Stamp Office, Room 222, Aidan House, All Saints Office Centre, Newcastle-upon-Tyne NE1 2BG

Nottingham : Stamp Office, Lower Ground Floor, Lambert House, Talbot Street, Nottingham NG1 5NN

Sheffield : Stamp Office, Revenue Buildings, 123 West Street, Sheffield S1 3SP

Appendix B

STAMP DUTY TABLES

**Table 1   Conveyances dated on or after 1 January 1892
but before 29 April 1910**

Consideration (price)	Duty
£25 or under	6d for every £5 or part thereof
over £25 but not exceeding £300	2s 6d for every £25 or part thereof
over £300	5s 0d for every £50 or part thereof

**Table 2   Conveyances dated on or after 29 April 1910
but before 1 August 1947**

Consideration (price)	Certified as not exceeding £500	No certificate
£25 or under	6d for every £5 or part thereof	1s 0d for every £5 or part thereof
over £25 but not exceeding £300	2s 6d for every £25 or part thereof	5s 0d for every £25 or part thereof
Over £300 but not exceeding £500	5s 0d for every £50 or part thereof	10s 0d for every £50 or part thereof
over £500	—	

Table 3 Conveyances dated on or after 1 August 1947 but before 10 July 1952

Consideration (price)	Certified as not exceeding £500	Certified as not exceeding £1500	Certified as not exceeding £1950	No certificate
£25 or under	6d for every £5 or part thereof	1s 0d for every £5 or part thereof		2s 0d for every £5 or part thereof
over £25 but not exceeding £300	2s 6d for every £25 or part thereof	5s 0d for every £25 or part thereof		10s 0d for every £25 or part thereof
over £300 but not exceeding £500	5s 0d for every £50 or part thereof	10s 0d for every £50 or part thereof		
over £500 but not exceeding £1500	—	10s 0d for every £50 or part thereof		£1 for every £50 or part thereof
over £1500 but not exceeding £1950	—	—	10s 0d for every £50 or part thereof PLUS £2 for every £50 or part thereof by which the consideration exceeds £1500	
over £1950	—	—	—	

Table 4 Conveyances dated on or after 10 July 1952 but before 1 August 1956

Consideration (price)	Certified as not exceeding £500	Certified as not exceeding £3000	Certified as not exceeding £3450	No certificate
under £25	6d for every £5 or part thereof	1s 0d for every £5 or part thereof	1s 6d for every £5 or part thereof	2s 0d for every £5 or part thereof
over £25 but not exceeding £300	2s 6d for every £25 or part thereof	5s 0d for every £25 or part thereof	7s 6d for every £25 or part thereof	10s 0d for every £25 or part thereof
over £300 but not exceeding £500	5s 0d for every £50 or part thereof	10s 0d for every £50 or part thereof	15s 0d for every £50 or part thereof	£1 for every £50 or part thereof
over £500 but not exceeding £3000	—	10s 0d for every £50 or part thereof	15s 0d for every £50 or part thereof	£1 for every £50 or part thereof
over £3000 but not exceeding £3450	—	—	15s 0d for every £50 or part thereof	£1 for every £50 or part thereof
over £3450	—	—	—	£1 for every £50 or part thereof

Table 5 Conveyances dated on or after 1 August 1956 but before 1 August 1958

Consideration (price)	Certified as not exceeding £3500	Certified as not exceeding £4250	Certified as not exceeding £5000	No certificate
£25 or under	6d for every £5 or part thereof	1s 0d for every £5 or part thereof	1s 6d for every £5 or part thereof	2s 0d for every £5 or part thereof
Over £25 but not exceeding £300	2s 6d for every £25 or part thereof	5s 0d for every £25 or part thereof	7s 6d for every £25 or part thereof	10s 0d for every £25 or part thereof
over £300 but not exceeding £3500	5s 0d for every £50 or part thereof	10s 0d for every £50 or part thereof	15s 0d for every £50 or part thereof	£1 for every £50 or part thereof
over £3500 but not exceeding £4250	—	10s 0d for every £50 or part thereof	15s 0d for every £50 or part thereof	£1 for every £50 or part thereof
over £4250 but not exceeding £5000	—	—	15s 0d for every £50 or part thereof	£1 for every £50 or part thereof
over £5000	—	—	—	£1 for every £50 or part thereof

Table 6 Conveyances dated on or after 1 August 1958 but before 1 August 1963

Consideration (price)	Certified as not exceeding £3500	Certified as not exceeding £4500	Certified as not exceeding £5250	Certified as not exceeding £6000	No certificate
£25 or under	nil	6d for every £5 or part thereof	1s 0d for every £5 or part thereof	1s 6d for every £5 or part thereof	2s 0d for every £5 or part thereof[1]
over £25 but not exceeding £300		2s 6d for every £50 or part thereof	5s 0d for every £25 or part thereof	7s 6d for every £25 or part thereof	10s 0d for every £25 or part thereof
over £300 but not exceeding £3500	—	5s 0d for every £25 or part thereof			
over £3500 but not exceeding £4500	—	—	10s 0d for every £50 or part thereof	15s 0d for every £50 or part thereof	
over £4500 but not exceeding £5250	—	—			
over £5250 but not exceeding £6000	—	—	—		
over £6000	—	—	—	—	£1 for every £50 or part thereof

[1] For Conveyances dated on or after 1/8/59, where the consideration was less than £5, the duty was 6d for every 25s 0d or part thereof.

Table 7 Conveyances dated on or after 1 August 1963 but before 1 August 1967

Consideration (price)	Certified as not exceeding £4500	Certified as not exceeding £6000	No certificate
£5 or under		3d for every £2 10s 0d or part thereof	3d for every 25s 0d or part thereof
over £5 but not exceeding £20		6d for every £5 or part thereof	1s 0d for every £5 or part thereof
over £20 but not exceeding £35		2s 6d duty	5s 0d duty
over £35 but not exceeding £60	nil	5s 0d duty	10s 0d duty
over £60 but not exceeding £80		7s 6d duty	15s 0d duty
over £80 but not exceeding £100		10s 0d duty	£1 duty
over £100 but not exceeding £300		2s 6d for every £25 or part thereof	5s 0d for every £25 or part thereof

Consideration (price)	Certified as not exceeding £4500	Certified as not exceeding £6000	No Certificate
over £300 but not exceeding £4500	—	5s 0d for every £50 or part thereof	10s 0d for every £50 or part thereof
over £4500 but not exceeding £6000	—		
over £6000		—	

Table 8   Conveyances dated on or after 1 August 1967 but before 1 August 1970

Consideration (price)	Certified as not exceeding £5500	Certified as not exceeding £7000	No certificate
£5 or under	nil	3d for every £2 10s or part thereof	3d for every 25s 0d or part thereof
over £5 but not exceeding £20		6d for every £5 or part thereof	1s 0d for every £5 or part thereof
over £20 but not exceeding £35		2s 6d duty	5s 0d duty
over £35 but not exceeding £60		5s 0d duty	10s 0d duty
over £60 but not exceeding £80		7s 6d duty	15s 0d duty
over £80 but not exceeding £100		10s 0d duty	£1 duty
over £100 but not exceeding £300		2s 6d for every £25 or part thereof	5s 0d for every £25 or part thereof

Consideration (price)	Certified as not exceeding £5500	Certified as not exceeding £7000	No Certificate
over £300 but not exceeding £5500		5s 0d for every £50 or part thereof	10s 0d for every £50 or part thereof
over £5500 but not exceeding £7000	—		
over £7000	—	—	

Table 9 Conveyances dated on or after 1 August 1970 but before 1 August 1972[1]

Consideration (price)	Certified as not exceeding £5500	Certified as not exceeding £7000	No certificate
£5 or under	nil	1s 0d duty	1s 0d duty
over £5 but not exceeding £100	nil	1s 0d for every £10 or part thereof	2s 0d for every £10 or part thereof
over £100 but not exceeding £300	nil	2s 0d for every £20 or part thereof	4s 0d for every £20 or part thereof
over £300 but not exceeding £5500	nil	5s 0d for every £50 or part thereof	10s 0d for every £50 or part thereof
over £5500 but not exceeding £7000	—	5s 0d for every £50 or part thereof	10s 0d for every £50 or part thereof
over £7000	—	—	10s 0d for every £50 or part thereof

[1] On or after 15 February 1971, references to 1s 0d, 2s 0d, 4s 0d, 5s 0d, and 10s 0d, are to be read as referring to their decimal equivalent, ie, 5, 10, 20, 25, and 50 new pence, respectively.

Table 10   Conveyances dated on or after 1 August 1972 but before 1 April 1974

Consideration (price)	Certified as not exceeding £10,000	Certified as not exceeding £15,000	No certificate
£5 or under	nil	5p duty	5p duty
over £5 but not exceeding £100	nil	5p for every £10 or part thereof	10p for every £10 or part thereof
over £100 but not exceeding £300	nil	10p for every £20 or part thereof	20p for every £20 or part thereof
over £300 but not exceeding £10,000	nil	25p for every £50 or part thereof	50p for every £50 or part thereof
over £10,000 but not exceeding £15,000	—	25p for every £50 or part thereof	50p for every £50 or part thereof
over £15,000	—	—	50p for every £50 or part thereof

Table 11   Conveyances dated on or after 1 April 1974

Consideration (price)	Certified as not exceeding £15,000	Certified as not exceeding £20,000	Certified as not exceeding £25,000	Certified as not exceeding £30,000	No certificate
£5 or under	nil	5p duty	5p duty	10p duty	10p duty
over £5 but not exceeding £100	nil	5p for every £10 or part thereof	10p for every £10 or part thereof	15p for every £10 or part thereof	20p for every £10 or part thereof
over £100 but not exceeding £300	nil	10p for every £20 or part thereof	20p for every £20 or part thereof	30p for every £20 or part thereof	40p for every £20 or part thereof
over £300 but not exceeding £15,000	—	25p for every £50 or part thereof	50p for every £50 or part thereof	75p for every £50 or part thereof	£1 for every £50 or part thereof
over £15,000 but not exceeding £20,000	—				
over £20,000 but not exceeding £25,000	—	—			
over £25,000 but not exceeding £30,000	—	—	—		
over £30,000	—	—	—	—	

Table A leases dated on or after 1 January 1892 but before 29 April 1910

(a) Duty on the rent reserved

Average annual rent	Term exceeding 35 years but not exceeding 100 years	Term exceeding 100 years
under £25	3s 0d for every £5 of rent or part thereof	6s 0d for every £5 of rent or part thereof
over £25 but not exceeding £100	15s 0d for every £25 of rent or part thereof	£1 10s 0d for every £25 of rent or part thereof
over £100	£1 10s 0d for every £50 of rent or part thereof	£3 for every £50 of rent or part thereof

PLUS
(b) Duty on any price paid for the grant of the lease

the same duty as for a conveyance at that price of the same date (see Table 1, page 155).

Table B leases dated on or after 29 April 1910 but before 1 August 1947

(a) Duty on the rent reserved

Average annual rent	Term exceeding 35 years but not exceeding 100 years	Term exceeding 100 years
under £25	6s 0d for every £5 of rent or part thereof	12s 0d for every £5 of rent or part thereof
over £25 but not exceeding £100	£1 10s 0d for every £25 of rent or part thereof	£3 for every £25 of rent or part thereof
over £100	£3 for every £50 of rent or part thereof	£6 for every £50 of rent or part thereof

PLUS
(b) Duty on any price paid for the grant of the lease

the same duty as for a conveyance at that price of the same date (apply Table 2, page 155)

NOTE that the reduced rate applicable where there was a certificate of value, could not be claimed for leases dated before 31/3/11 and, in any event, could not be claimed if the rent exceeded £20 per annum. (In such cases, use the 'No certificate' column.)

Table C leases dated on or after 1 August 1947
but before 1 August 1963

(a) Duty on the rent reserved

Average annual rent	Term exceeding 35 years but not exceeding 100 years	Term exceeding 100 years
under £25	12s 0d for every £5 of rent or part thereof	£1 4s 0d for every £5 of rent or part thereof
over £25 but not exceeding £100	£3 for every £25 of rent or part thereof	£6 for every £25 of rent or part thereof
over £100	£6 for every £50 of rent or part thereof	£12 for every £50 of rent or part thereof

PLUS
(b) Duty on any price paid for the grant of the lease

the same duty as for a conveyance at that price of the same date (see Tables 3-6, pages 156-9).

NOTE that the reduced rates applicable where the deed contained a certificate of value, could not be claimed if the rent exceeded £20 pa (in the case of leases dated before 1/8/58), or £50 pa (in the case of leases dated on or after that date). In such cases, use the 'No certificate' column.

Table D leases dated on or after 1 August 1963 but before 1 April 1974[1]

(a) Duty on the rent reserved

Average annual rent	Term exceeding 35 years but not exceeding 100 years	Term exceeding 100 years
under £25	6s 0d for every £5 of rent or part thereof	12s 0d for every £5 of rent or part thereof
over £25 but not exceeding £100	£1 10s 0d for every £25 of rent or part thereof	£3 for every £25 of rent or part thereof
over £100	£3 for every £50 of rent or part thereof	£6 for every £50 of rent or part thereof

[1] On or after 15 February 1971, references to 6s 0d, 10s 0d, and 12s 0d, are to be read as referring to their decimal equivalent, ie, 30, 50, and 60 new pence, respectively.

PLUS

(b) Duty on any price paid for the grant of the lease

the same duty as for a conveyance at that price of the same date (see Tables 7-10, pages 160-5).

NOTE that the reduced rates applicable where the deed contained a certificate of value, could not be claimed where the rent exceeded £50 pa (in the case of leases dated before 1/8/72), or £150 pa (in the case of leases dated on or after that date). In such cases, use the 'No certificate' column.

Table E leases dated on or after 1 April 1974

(a) Duty on the rent reserved

Average annual rent	Term exceeding 35 years but not exceeding 100 years	Term exceeding 100 years
under £25	60p for every £5 of rent or part thereof	£1.20 for every £5 of rent or part thereof
over £25 but not exceeding £100	£3 for every £25 of rent or part thereof	£6 for every £25 of rent or part thereof
over £100	£6 for every £50 of rent or part thereof	£12 for every £50 of rent or part thereof

PLUS

(b) Duty on any price paid for the grant of the lease

the same duty as for a conveyance at that price of the same date (see Table 11, page 166).

NOTE that the reduced rates applicable where the deed contained a certificate of value, could not be claimed where the rent exceeded £150 pa. In such cases, use the 'No certificate' column.

Acknowledgements

My thanks go to my colleagues, Priscilla Sarton, Paul Butt, and others, for allowing me to draw on their considerable knowledge of conveyancing law and practice, and for their most valuable comments on the text.

All official forms appearing in this book are reproduced with the kind permission of the Controller of HM Stationery Office, and the Chief Land Registrar.

Index